TESTIMONIALS

"Rob, I just finished reading your book, and I want to say I am very proud of you. Your passion for excelling in your field, for serving and helping people (for whom Christ died), and your love for Christ shine brightly through the pages. Your book was an educational, motivational, practical, personal, and an insightful window into the world of a doctor who wants to excel. It is a must read for everyone in the medical field. Well done, brother!"

—Pastor John W. Minnema, senior pastor, Hawthorne Gospel Church

"Dr. Kayal is the quintessential surgeon, teacher, and family man. He is driven by his faith and has stayed the same magnanimous person I met in 2010. He inspires those who work with him to be the best they can be, and not just as surgeons but in life as well. I am proud to call him my friend."

—Jeff Pope, MD, FAAOS, orthopaedic surgeon, chief,
Sports Medicine Service, Kayal Orthopaedic Center

"Dr. Kayal provides meaningful and spirited insight here on what many consider elusive keys to success that he has mastered. His firebrand approach to delivering the highest quality patient care based upon passionate clinical devotion to orthopaedics is remarkable. Dr. Kayal's relentless devotion to his practice, and those that have been privileged to be a part of his journey in medicine, is truly inspiring—matched only by his sincerity to the pursuit of excellence. A must read for those entering the field of medicine. Well done."

—Keith J. Roberts, Esq., partner, Brach Eichler, LLC

"Brother, you truly add so much more to my life with your genuine love. I want you to know that often when I talk to my children about success, I'll bring you up as an example, and it's not measured by the financial securities that you have. Rather, it is measured by the level of passion that you approach life. You exude that every moment of your life. You're passionate when you love someone, you're passionate when you do work, you're passionate when you approach any subject in life, and that fire in your heart lights up your skies and reveals so much beauty that all can see. I am truly so fortunate to know you as a human being. You are incredible. I love you. I am always so happy to see you and be with you."

—Manaf Saker, DMD, oral surgeon, Ridgewood Oral Surgery

"A very comprehensive but easily readable guide to success for the neophyte orthopaedist. I have had the privilege of knowing and working with Rob Kayal for his entire professional career. His story epitomizes the dedication, commitment, and hard work that it takes to become an outstanding physician. Dr. Kayal's guide walks you through the path of achieving fiscal security while maintaining one's integrity in the highly competitive world of orthopaedic practice."

—Edward C. Friedland, MD, FAAOS, FACS, orthopaedic surgeon, Kayal Orthopaedic Center

"It has truly been an honor and privilege to work alongside Dr. Kayal and the entire organization. I have seen firsthand how Dr. Kayal has been able to continuously transform this practice year after year and consistently stay one step ahead of the rest. To witness his intelligence, energy, charisma, and passion every single day has been awe-inspiring, and it is with sincere gratitude that I can say I have been blessed to be a part of this journey and learn from him."

—Amit Sood, MD, FAAOS, orthopaedic surgeon, chief, Shoulder Service, Kayal Orthopaedic Center

"Thank you is never sufficient. I can't express enough how incredibly blessed I feel to be part of your team. I will never be able to repay you for the incredible care and kindness you have given to my family. My family is my whole world; nothing is more precious. You have continuously made sure my family was taken care of. You are beyond amazing. Your depth of love and kindness to everyone you encounter is so extraordinary. God truly blessed this world when He created you. I am forever grateful to have crossed your path in this life."

—Antoniette Napolitano, office manager, Kayal Orthopaedic Center

"This book should be required reading for every premedical/medical student and resident. Thank you so much again for sharing it with me. Every time I come back to review it, I am amazed all over again by all the incredible insights it provides, covering all the different aspects of the practice and life. Written by Dr. Kayal, who came, saw, and conquered the field both personally and professionally, this book shares his invaluable knowledge on how to be a truly great doctor, businessman, and human being."

—Edward A. Lin, MD, FAAOS, orthopaedic surgeon, chief, Hand Service, Kayal Orthopaedic Center

"Dr. Kayal, I was hired by you (yes, you when you did the hiring back in the day) at the young age of nineteen, and here I am twelve and a half years later. I am still utterly amazed at what an outstanding surgeon, boss, leader, father, and now "Gido" you are! The list could go on and on. You are someone to look up to. You took the tiny Ridgewood office on Maple Avenue and rapidly grew before everyone's eyes, always making your patients the top priority. You are overly generous to your staff and equally put us as a top priority. I've seen you not only surgically and conservatively treat every patient's problem that walks through the doors of the office, but I have even seen you firsthand save patients' lives when other doctors have failed them or misdiagnosed them. I am so proud to be an employee of yours and have been able to experience this growth you've accomplished. Here's to many more years of success!

—Candice Binkunski, surgical coordinator
manager, Kayal Orthopaedic Center

"An inspiring and insightful 'secret-revealing' book from a successful and hardworking good man. I am lucky to learn from and work with Dr. Kayal."

—Klodian Xurre, director of Kayal Medical
Imaging, Kayal Orthopaedic Center

"Dr. Kayal goes above and beyond describing how to successfully navigate this new world in health care. It is an excellent read and on point. As a provider and owner of a multidisciplinary office with over thirty years of experience, I can wholeheartedly agree with everything outlined in this book! I ran my practice like this for the past thirty-three years. I totally agree with everything he stated and was bold enough to put in writing and share with us. It takes a strong work ethic, as well as empathy for your patients to excel and stand out. I am happy to have merged my practice with Kayal Orthopaedic Center. I could not have picked a better organization to work for. Dr. Kayal, you are my RWJBarnabas Health. You are inspiring, and it is a pleasure to be part of the team!"

—Dr. Paul Francis Marston, certified chiropractic
sports physician, Kayal Orthopaedic Center

"I distinctly remember meeting Dr. Kayal for the first time nearly twenty years ago on a Saturday when my youngest son, Connor, then six years old and in the first grade, fractured his tibia in a peewee football game. We went to the emergency room where a coworker's wife happened to be the on-duty x-ray tech. I asked if she knew a good orthopaedist, and she recommended a young doctor named Robert Kayal, who coincidentally lived in the same town where her husband and I worked as police officers. She gave me his business card and the plan was to contact his office first thing Monday for an appointment. After a long day in the emergency room, my wife took Connor home, leg in a cast, and I reported to work where I was scheduled to work the nightshift. This is where the story goes off the rails a bit.

At approximately 10 or 11 p.m., I received a frantic phone call from my wife that something was wrong with Connor. He had been up crying for hours in excruciating pain and she didn't know what to do. Feeling desperate, I violated department policy and looked up Dr. Kayal's personal contact information from our in-house computer, and then I called him at home (before cell phones). I remember his wife, Kim, answering the phone and asking her not to call the police on this deranged person calling their home in the middle of the night, as I would probably be the responding officer anyway.

When Dr. Kayal got on the phone, I introduced myself and explained the situation. Instead of immediately hanging up on me and applying for a restraining order, he explained that he was also a parent and compassionately listened and provided guidance. However, it wasn't until the following morning when Dr. Kayal *called us* to check on Connor that I realized what a special doctor and extraordinary person he was. The fact is I was just some stranger who called his home in the middle of the night (totally inappropriate), and my son wasn't even his patient, yet he took time out of his Sunday to call and check on him. How many other doctors would do that?

Dr. Kayal, you probably don't even remember this story because you've touched so many people in this way, but I will never forget what you did for my family on that night nearly twenty years ago and countless times since. You've not only become our family doctor, but I'm blessed to also call you my friend."

—Robert Lyon, director of operations, Kayal Orthopaedic Center

"Thank you for sharing your thoughts and writing a very informative and inspiring book. Many of the sections relate to my world in human resources. Thank you for your wisdom, leadership, and respect of everyone. I am blessed to know and work with you."

—Maida Garabed, director of human
resources, Kayal Orthopaedic Center

"Writing a book is something few people accomplish, and even fewer write one with as much experience, wisdom, and inspiration packed into it as yours. Amazing work!"

—Paul Bagi, MD, FAAOS, orthopaedic surgeon,
chief, Spine Service, Kayal Orthopaedic Center

"Thank you for always sharing your wisdom, knowledge, and continued teaching. As you said in your book, 'Choose medicine for the right reasons.' Well, you actually did. The operating room is your happy place. Fixing patients' orthopaedic conditions gives you the most gratification. You work tirelessly and the hardest out of everyone in this practice. You have taught me medicine and treated the physician assistants like doctors. Through your teaching and training, you have made sure we provide the same quality of care as a doctor would. Essentially, we all became your direct extensions. But most importantly, you have been teaching me about Jesus Christ (عيسى عليه السلام). I have truly enjoyed our religious discussions and the stories (e.g., the parable of the lost son). This has been the highlight of my career at Kayal Orthopaedic Center."

—Roya Rahimi, PA-C, CNMT, physician
assistant, Kayal Orthopaedic Center

"You are a *beacon of light!* God has given you many talents. You know how to put them to use and multiply the gifts given to you and share with the world, inviting each one to the light. Hence, you and your beautiful wife and beautiful children are under *divine protection and guidance.* It's an honor to see the glory of God through you, your family, and this practice. I am not being sweet; it is the *truth!* Thank you, Dr. Kayal!"

—Esmerelda Mena, director of business
development, Kayal Orthopaedic Center

"Robert, this was a remarkable read. I especially liked your points on the Seven C's. However, I believe that one of the major differences in medicine is the iPhone. I can remember for so long having something on my beltline that would beep me a telephone number, generally from an emergency room where there were elderly physicians who were not board certified and had a patient who needed to be seen late at night or early in the morning. We had to go. We had to examine the patient ourselves and then call in the specialist if we needed them. In addition, there were so few specialists then that we had to do so much on our own (spinal taps, CVP lines, spinal taps, liver biopsies, etc.). Moreover, one was a physician twenty-four hours a day, every day. There were no part-time physicians. There was nobody who said it was five o'clock and it was not their time when a patient called. We were on call several nights a week. We even made house calls with all our specialties, but that stopped for me and most others in 1977 when in Paterson, Dr. David Doktor was killed making a house call in the early evening. So for me practicing medicine under the atmosphere today is remarkably different. I'm so thankful that I have so much support, so many young people to help with the hardware and software. Although, I should mention, forty years ago I was the first group to start to bill on the computer, send out appointments through the computer, and have an MBA run the multispecialty group I headed. Most people don't want to hear how much dedication and so much of our lives was given to medicine. It was all-consuming. I was on call every night. This is something that is hard to appreciate with the way you run the group so marvelously so that people can practice their talents, skills, and healing but have time with their family. We see patients on the same day if they have an emergency and provide the most excellent care that's available while at the same time having time for learning and teaching. But most of all, seeing our children grow. One last point that you spend time on is how important it is to give the physicians training in economics. Thanks for writing this. I think that this should be a standard read for those starting early. This is from an oldie but a goodie who would do it all over again as it has been a great and proud journey to be called a healer."

—Alan Zalkowitz, MD, rheumatologist, chief, Department of Rheumatology, Kayal Rheumatology Center

"First and foremost, I want to congratulate you on this achievement. Secondly, I'd like to express my gratitude for sharing your heart, knowledge, and experiences with us. Your book brought tears to my eyes. Reading your book transported me back to my childhood. As I grew older, I saw my parents work extremely hard. They used to work long hours, sometimes until late at night. I witnessed them being steadfast and disciplined, and as a result, they accomplished many things that benefited our family (good times). And as you say, God is the head of the house, and a house cannot stand without Him. Thank you for sharing once more. You are a true inspiration. May God always bless you and your family."

—Jeannette Rivera, director of chiropractic and physical therapy, Kayal Orthopaedic Center

"Dr. Kayal, I really enjoyed reading your book. I thank you for sharing the salient attributes of a successful orthopaedic surgeon and successful businessman who has developed a center of excellence that stands above other organizations. I also believe that having a strong core of religion and family complements our profession and allows for growth and prosperity. These characteristics keep us well-rounded, as eloquently described in your book."

—Patricia Donohue, ACNP, chief, Disorders of Bone Metabolism, Kayal Orthopaedic Center

"Hi Dr. Kayal, I wanted to send this message to give you your flowers on a job well done with the book. It was great to learn more about your come-up, especially the part about having kids during residency! Your values of God first, family, and then work is a philosophy I'm glad you touched upon to remind everyone. You're someone I look up to. Seeing what you've done from an entrepreneurial aspect of your business and the items you accentuated in this book are noted for my own endeavors. Keep up the great work."

—Benjamin Rodriguez, territory manager, Theragen Spine

"Dr. Kayal, I just finished reading your book this morning. I enjoyed it tremendously. Being someone who loves medicine, business, and technology, your perspective and personal experience are oddly relatable. Of course, I am not a physician, but the theme is relatable. I am an athletic trainer and I've always strived to be excellent. That's the theme I kept hearing and feeling. Strive to be excellent whether with faith, family, or business. Thank you!"

—Joshua Jimenez, LAT, ATC

Mastering
The Business of Medicine &
The Doctor-Patient
Relationship

From Solo
Practice
Entrepreneur To
Orthopaedic
Empire

Robert A. Kayal, MD, FAAOS, FAAHKS

WESTBOW
PRESS®
A DIVISION OF THOMAS NELSON
& ZONDERVAN

WestBow Press books may be ordered through booksellers or by contacting:

WestBow Press
A Division of Thomas Nelson & Zondervan
1663 Liberty Drive
Bloomington, IN 47403
www.westbowpress.com
844-714-3454

ISBN: 979-8-3850-2389-9 (sc)
ISBN: 979-8-3850-2390-5 (hc)
ISBN: 979-8-3850-2573-2 (e)

Library of Congress Control Number: 2024910056

Print information available on the last page.

WestBow Press rev. date: 05/17/2024

CONTENTS

To the love of my life, my wife, Kim S. Kayal, RN, of twenty-nine years, and to our six beautiful children—Katlyn Madeline, Michaela Noel, Robert Joseph, Shannon Isabella, Mia Grace, and Luke Christopher—all gifts and blessings from our awesome Triune God above. This book is dedicated in their honor because of the sacrifices they have made over the years so that I could share my love, time, commitment, and passion for the field of orthopaedic surgery with my patients and colleagues at Kayal Orthopaedic Center. I hope and pray that these sacrifices were not made in vain but rather that others could benefit, in some way, from my orthopaedic intervention and care over the years.

ACKNOWLEDGMENTS

There are so many that come to mind as I write this book and think about how many people have supported me over the past twenty-five years. So many family members, friends, health care providers and professional colleagues enjoyed this beautiful journey alongside me over those same years. Some came along for the whole ride, and others for just some part of it. However, each has played such an instrumental role in my personal, spiritual, and/ or professional life.

First and foremost, I must say that all my thanks, praise, worship, honor, and glory belong to my awesome Triune God—God the Father, God the Son, and God the Holy Spirit—the omniscient, omnipresent, and omnipotent God from whom all blessings flow.

Secondly, I would like to thank my nuclear family. To Kim S. Kayal, RN, my "right hand woman," I say, "Thank you from the bottom of my heart, honey. You have loved, supported, and encouraged me since the first day we met when I was just a medical student, and you were the nurse caring for a mutual patient of ours." Kim, the mother of our six children, has been my backbone my entire career and the "behind the scenes" V12 quad-turbo engine that has helped to drive this beast of a practice for all these years. I, of course, also want to thank our six wonderful children, all blessings from God—Katlyn Madeline, Michaela Noel, Robert

Joseph, Shannon Isabella, Mia Grace, and Luke Christopher—for their never-ending love for me and for the sacrifices they've all made over the years so that I could serve my profession and patients wholeheartedly. All of this is for all of you. It has always been, and will always be, for you all.

I am eternally grateful, also, to my loving mother, Nadia, and late father, Michael, both of whom supported me through college and through medical school so that I could pursue my lifelong dream of becoming an orthopaedic surgeon. I would never have been able to do this without their love, encouragement, and support. I could never thank them enough for the way they loved me, cared for me, guided me, and directed me my entire life and for sacrificing everything for me and their five other children so that my siblings and I could enjoy a better life than they ever could. I will always feel indebted to my parents for giving me this opportunity to get educated and to make something of myself, and I will never stop singing your praises. My mission in life was to always make you proud, and I am so sorry for the times when I have failed.

I am also so thankful for my five loving brothers and sisters, some of whom I have been blessed to work with over the years. One in particular is my brother Mike, my chief physician assistant, whom I am so grateful to continue to work alongside today, and for the past almost fifteen years as well. These have been the greatest brothers and sisters that anyone could ever hope for. Thank you all for the life that we've enjoyed together all these years. I so look forward to what's ahead and to living out the rest of our lives together, with our own children and grandchildren, as family.

I would like to also thank the hundreds of incredible employees of mine, both my medical and nonmedical staff, who have worked tirelessly to contribute to the growth and success of Kayal

Orthopaedic Center since day one. I'm so thankful for our team of unbelievably highly trained health care providers that have cared for our community of patients over the years. I could not have done any of this without each of you, and I will never forget the impact you have had on the practice. I will never forget all the emails and cards I've received about all of you, and I still have all of them to this day. I know I've said it repeatedly, but you all have been such a tremendous blessing in my life. Thank you all for choosing to work at Kayal Orthopaedic Center and to help care for all of these wonderful patients year after year.

I am sincerely indebted to my team of professionals who have supported me in one way or another over the years as well. From my accountant, Jeff Harrison, CPA, who has been with me from day one, to my team of health care attorneys, especially Michael Schaff, Esq., and Keith Roberts, Esq., to my graphic designers, Dan Antonelli and his amazing team of brand builders at KickCharge, to my friends Jude Pagano and Thomas Green from Clear Channel Outdoor and numerous other media groups that have helped me advertise and market the brand year after year, and finally, to my loyal referral sources that have supported Kayal Orthopaedic Center since its inception. Each and every one of you has helped this practice become what it is today, and I will never, ever, ever forget you.

I am so thankful to my two favorite pastors, the late Dr. Charles F. Stanley from In Touch Ministries and Pastor John W. Minnema from my home church, Hawthorne Gospel Church, both of whom, more than anyone else on the planet, have helped me to better understand and interpret the Word of God found in the Holy Bible. Knowing you both and being your student for almost thirty years has made me a better child of God, husband, father, and physician.

The impact that you have made on my life, and the lives of my family members and others, will transcend generations. As such, I will forever be indebted to both of you.

I would like to thank RWJBarnabas Health, especially Mark Manigan, Esq., John Doll, Deb Lienhardt, Esq., Don Callahan, MBA, FACMPE, and Frank Goldstein, MBA, for believing in me and for being my "Shark." When you made that investment in me and the practice, I promised that I would never, ever, ever let you down. That promise still stands, and I am committed, now even more than ever, to ensuring that Kayal Orthopaedic Center will forever be the best investment in your portfolio.

Finally, I would be remiss if I failed to thank the thousands and thousands of patients who have afforded me the opportunity, honor, privilege, and blessing to care for them over the years. Yes, that's correct. I have always considered, and will always consider, it an honor, privilege, and blessing to be entrusted with your orthopaedic care and to be called your doctor. Thank you, from the bottom of my heart, for affording me that privilege. My life's work has been dedicated to making sure that I don't fail you.

PREFACE

On January 7, 1968, I was born at St. Joseph's Hospital in Paterson, New Jersey, to Mr. Michael and Mrs. Nadia Kayal. My father was a very successful and accomplished electrical engineer, and my mother chose to stay at home to raise her children. My parents ultimately had six children, three boys and three girls. I was the third child. Although my father was born in the United States, his parents, my mother, and my mother's parents all emigrated to the United States of America from Aleppo, Syria. All were Syrian Christians. My patriotic father willingly chose to serve in the United States Navy for four years immediately after earning his high school diploma and then, based on the guidance and direction of the United States Navy, pursued his bachelor of science degree in electrical engineering. After earning this degree, my dad became an electrical engineer and continued to excel in this profession his entire work life, ultimately becoming the highest ranked electrical engineer at his company, with many others under his charge. My mother, who could barely speak English at first, stayed at home to raise, care for, love, and nurture their six children.

As one can imagine, it would be very difficult to raise six children and put them all through college and me through medical school on an engineer's salary. But they did it. They did it through self-sacrifice and other business investments I watched my parents participate in my entire childhood. They did what they had to do to achieve their goal, and that was to provide for their children and to ensure that we had a better life and future than either of them had for themselves.

I watched my parents enjoy a vigorous but healthy balance of their personal and professional lives. They did everything for us. We enjoyed such an awesome childhood. I watched them work hard but also noticed that they never missed any of our after-school sporting events. They were always at our soccer games and baseball games. We went to church every single Sunday, and then Sunday school immediately thereafter. We spent so much time with our nuclear family but with our extended family as well. Mom prepared dinner so that we could all eat together every night. Afterward, she would make her kids' six school lunches for the next day. We went on vacations every year, but they always lived within their means. All eight of us would go down the shore, packed into our station wagon, and either stayed in motels or on camping grounds in our pop-up camper. My parents were strict, but only out of love. It's what I call today "tough love." Because of it, we learned to never curse, and to always respect our elders. They taught us traditional, old-school values, which I still share today.

In short, I watched my parents work hard but simultaneously love us, sacrifice for us, care for us, and provide for us. My parents taught us good manners, proper etiquette, strong work ethic, how to treat people, how to love others as ourselves, to fear the Lord, and the importance of our spiritual life. They instilled in us the importance of faith, family, education, and work, and in that order. These values are still of utmost importance in my life.

Because of my upbringing, like most of us, I became like my parents. I wanted to do the same things for my future children that my parents did for me. As such, I began my mission to emulate them.

I went to church and Sunday school each week. I paid attention to the prayers, sermons, and Bible readings as I really wanted to learn the Word of God. I worked so hard in school, in sports, and at various jobs in my younger years, and did quite well in all, thank God. I entered the workforce at such a young age, too. I always held jobs as far back as I can remember. For instance, my siblings and I had paper routes for so many years during our elementary and middle school years. Everyone in the neighborhood knew the hardworking Kayal kids. These were the days when we had to manually put the newspapers together, pile them up in newspaper carrier bags held on our shoulders, or pack them on the bike racks or into baskets on the backs of our bicycles. We then would have to deliver them to all our customers and collect our fee from them once a week just to be reimbursed for the price of the newspapers we delivered. Keep in mind we *only* profited if our customers were kind, compassionate, and gracious enough to consider tipping us. We survived on tips alone. Yes, I know what you're thinking and you're right. Some of our customers would fall weeks behind in our collecting efforts, asking us to "please come back next week" or, worse yet, would never even consider tipping us at all. Nevertheless, I'll never forget how our mom sacrificed for us every Sunday morning when we were younger. You see, on Sundays, the papers were just massive—so thick and so heavy! That's because the papers had to be manually stuffed with all the coupons and circulars from the local advertisers and stores. Well, guess who had to stuff those papers every Sunday morning. We did! We had to assemble them, stuff them, and then deliver them to over one hundred households. The newspapers were so massive and so heavy that our mom could not bear to even watch us attempt to do this ourselves. As such, in her loving-kindness, good-natured, and sacrificial ways, she would drive us to the assembly station every Sunday at 5:30 a.m. where she would then help us stuff and pack all the newspapers to be delivered. Then my brothers, sisters, and I would hop onto the back of the opened tailgate of our Ford Country Squire station wagon while our mom would drive house to house allowing us to team up and deliver the more than one hundred newspapers to our customers on our various paper routes. Keep in mind that after all this, we had to get back home, shower, change for church, and somehow make it to church by 9 a.m. every Sunday morning. Somehow, some way, likely by God's divine intervention, every Sunday morning we were able to get to church on time.

In addition to my paper route responsibilities, I always mowed lawns, raked leaves, shoveled driveways in the snow, babysat, and worked at gyms and gas stations during my entire childhood. I did anything and everything I could to emulate my parents and to be like them. Then, thanks to my parents, I was blessed with the ability to go away to college where I again worked so hard to receive my bachelor of science in premedicine degree. I always worked in college, too, by the way. Fortunately, because I excelled in college, I was immediately accepted into medical school and graduated four years later with honors. After this, I applied to, and was accepted into, the coveted and extremely competitive field of orthopaedic surgery. During these next five years, I served first as resident physician, then senior resident physician, and then finally chief resident physician in the department of orthopaedic surgery.

During those extremely rigorous five years of orthopaedic surgery training in New York, I was considered by many to be an outlier. People thought I was out of my mind. You see, because of the nature of the exhausting and rigorous residency training program, residents were supposed to live close to the training program that they were accepted into. Well, I just couldn't, because in my first year of training, I married a nurse who worked in New Jersey. Therefore, we chose to settle in Englewood Cliffs, New Jersey, during those years, as it was about halfway between our two work destinations. For five years, my wife would go one way to get to work in New Jersey and I would go the other way and cross two bridges to report to duty in New York City and/or Long Island. In addition, we had kids during my residency. Most residents wait until they're done with this part of their education because it's too hard to manage both the requirements of the residency program and a spouse—let alone kids!

You see, in those days, before the law changed in New York, we worked thirty-six-hour shifts, and because we lost one of our three orthopaedic residents in my first year of residency, the other orthopaedic resident and I were left to work thirty-six-hour shifts every other night, instead of every third night, during our training. What that meant is we would start rounding at 5 a.m. one day and would not leave the hospital until 5 p.m. the next day. Often, we did not sleep a wink during those thirty-six hours because emergency room visits for orthopaedic problems just kept coming. We were certainly thrown in with the wolves. We saw everything. We received such incredible training, and I couldn't have asked for a better experience. It is what developed my confidence and abilities as an orthopaedic surgeon. It was a killer, but I did it. People thought I had lost my mind living in New Jersey with this hectic and exhausting lifestyle, but I didn't care. I just did what I had to do. That's all I knew. You just do what you have to do to succeed.

Well, unfortunately, as this was not enough, the commute to and from work was often one to two hours in traffic each way. There was no rest for the weary. Well, for those five years, I took advantage of every second I was in my car. I would listen to books on tapes or on

CDs every single day in that bumper-to-bumper traffic, both going to work and returning. I went through the entire Holy Bible a few times and so many orthopaedic textbooks as well. I learned so much about my Heavenly Father God, His Son Jesus, and the Holy Spirit that dwells within every believer. I learned so much about every facet of orthopaedics as well. Those car rides day after day after day made me a better child of God, husband, father, and orthopaedic surgeon as well. I will *never* forget those days and what I learned during that time.

Well, I finally finished my orthopaedic training in May 1999. It was comprehensive, challenging, painful, demanding, grueling, and outstanding all at the same time. I learned so much during my five years of training. I learned about orthopaedic basis science, inpatient and outpatient care, general orthopaedics, spine care, pediatric orthopaedics, sports medicine and arthroscopy, joint replacement surgery, trauma, fracture care, musculoskeletal oncology, hand and upper extremity, as well as foot and ankle surgery. I had such an incredible experience and finished feeling so confident because of the high volume of surgeries that I had performed in my training. As such, on July 1, 1999, I went into practice in Bergen County, New Jersey, and I have remained here in practice ever since. The rest is history, and this book will tell you how I did it and how that history was made.

INTRODUCTION

I have wanted to write a book about the business of medicine for a long time now. "Why?", you ask. The reason is because I have witnessed so many tragic changes in the medical profession over the years. Changes that could have been avoided if doctors and other health care providers only had a clue about running a successful medical business. Yes, I said "medical *business*" not "medical practice."

I have seen so many doctors give up, switch careers, or sell out to large conglomerates of health care employers because the physicians and clinicians were not able to succeed on their own or in a small group. I must be honest; it has really been so hard to watch. The fact of the matter is that the business of medicine is not taught in, or part of, the medical school curriculums. As such, these poor health care providers just went into the profession blind. They had no idea what to expect. There was no guidance or direction provided during their training. There was just ignorance and naiveté when they came out into the world. They were left to figure it out for themselves and just told to flap their wings and try to fly.

The problem is that most businesses fail, and the business of medicine is not immune to this. Especially if you have no idea what to expect and you have no guidance or direction and you're just thrown in with the wolves. It still blows my mind that medicine, as a business, is not taught in medical school.

Well, I want to change that. I think it should be. In fact, I think it must be, and I'm on a mission to make it happen. In medical school, unfortunately, there are no business courses. There are no courses about business ethics, etiquette, people skills, public speaking, finance, quantitative skills, marketing, strategy, brand management, leadership, entrepreneurship, management of technology and operations, accounting, billing, collections, accounts receivable, accounts payable, banking, wealth management, money management, budgeting, investments, economics, business management, human resources, etc. All these courses should be required.

My goal is to make this book mandatory reading material on every health care provider's curriculum. My hope is that some medical school dean or health care administrator gets ahold of this book, reads it, and decides to make it part of his or her teaching curriculum and training program. It will not only teach you how to succeed in the business of medicine, but it will also teach you how to succeed in medicine as well.

CHAPTER 1

MD

Medical doctor—MD. I may be a bit biased, but don't those letters after one's name just exude and command a certain degree of power, prestige, accomplishment, and respect? I mean, doesn't everyone's mother and father want their son or daughter to marry someone who makes a lot of money, is smart, and has a powerful, prestigious, and respectable occupation? After all, what do most parents say to their kids who are looking for the spouse of their dreams? "Do you really want to marry him or her? I'd really love to see you end up with a doctor or a lawyer." But they always say doctor first, don't they?

Or at least they used to.

Medicine has changed over the years. It used to be that the field of medicine was only for the exceptional. Those who were privileged to be accepted into this discipline typically scored in the top percentiles on their standardized tests and had GPAs that hovered around 4.0. These applicants also went to the top schools in the nation and excelled at everything. And I mean *everything*. Often, they were star athletes in high school or college, participated in lots of extracurricular activities, spoke numerous languages, participated in tons of medical research, engaged in missionary trips and volunteer activities at hospitals and medical institutions, and showed a devout interest in medicine from day one. Many spent summers and college breaks shadowing physicians just to learn the trade and demonstrate their passion for the field. Their letters of recommendation from esteemed health care professionals and other high-profile citizens stood out way above the rest. Medicine was only for the best and the brightest. The crème de la crème, we say. Now instead (and just ask my son, Robbie), trying to get into the fields of investment banking and/or private equity is like this. Medicine, not so much. Although there is still a great emphasis on earning an excellent GPA and MCAT score, it seems that, more recently, there has been an even greater emphasis on extracurricular activities and the "soft skills" of the applicants. Yes, according to the AAMC, the average GPA for matriculants was 3.75 and the average MCAT score was 512 in 2022–2023, but many admission panels are focusing more and more on things such as research, leadership roles, and applicant participation in volunteer work.

"Why was it this way?" you ask. Why was getting admission into medical school so competitive? Well, of course, it was because of all the things that the incredible field of medicine had to offer—power, prestige, autonomy, reward, the enjoyment of the coveted doctor-patient relationship, and of course, generous income, just to name a few.

A lot, but not all, has changed since then.

POWER

Nowadays, much to my distress, physicians have much less power to enjoy and quarterback the prized doctor-patient relationship. Often, we are at the mercy of insurance companies and payers. We cannot always just do what we feel is best for our patients. We used to be able to, but not anymore. We now must satisfy "medical necessity" requirements before preauthorizations can be obtained to proceed with care. Doctors used to spend so much time just talking to our patients, forging this proverbial doctor-patient relationship. They were the good old days. We would know everything about our patients, and they would know a lot about us too. We knew about one another's spouse, kids, vacations, occupations, hobbies, and so forth, and we certainly knew everything about their medical conditions, medical histories, medications, allergies, and surgical and social histories. We spent quality face-to-face time with one another, forming a bond of trust between us. Then, much to my chagrin, came the mandate for electronic medical records. Since then, bureaucrats and insurance companies have been forcing us to spend more time face-to-face with a computer monitor rather than with a patient. Since then, we must document, document, document—everything! "If it's not documented," we're told, "it wasn't done." Check this box. Then that one. Do this and then that. Meanwhile, the patient is staring at the backs of our heads as we act like clerks instead of physicians. We must play by the rules, or we won't get paid by the insurance companies. We can't prescribe this or that without trying this or that first. We need to do at least six weeks or eighteen visits of physical therapy before getting the proposed surgical procedure authorized. You need to try this before you can offer that. You must follow the payer's policy and procedure guidelines, or your services rendered will not be reimbursed. We are at their mercy. And to boot, the payers may still opt to deny payment for whatever reason they give, and then we waste so much time, effort, and expense paying employees to fight with them to get paid for the services we already provided to our patients. My head is spinning just writing this. All of this to say that this never-ending rigmarole is distracting from our ability, as physicians, to establish and maintain a high level of trust, commitment, and loyalty in this treasured doctor-patient relationship.

PRESTIGE

Furthermore, the field of medicine, in general, is much less prestigious than it used to be. In the past, what the physician (with whom patients enjoyed a trusting relationship) said was gospel. Patients listened to us and respected us, and the profession, much more than they do now. It was a different era. That was the old-school mentality, but that's the one that I know, cherish, admire, and respect. That was the one I was raised with. I love old-school. I don't like this new-school mentality that has made its way across the country and has become mainstream in our youth and younger adults, especially over the last twenty years. Unfortunately, there seems to be so many with baseline disrespectful and rude attitudes and general dispositions as their norm. There's no class. No etiquette. What happened to this country? How did the parents allow this? Then on top of this, largely due to the immediate access of medical information through "Dr. Google," patients are much more educated about their conditions, and they question their physicians much more than they used to. Sometimes this is a good thing, but most of the time it's not, because the questioning comes with attitude and a lack of trust. That doctor-patient bond was just never made. As such, patients often go for second and third opinions, which is a good thing. But if, God forbid, there is a difference of opinions between these different physicians, some patients don't hesitate to bash the more aggressive doctor on social media and in online reviews after siding with the more conservative one, even though it may just be a difference in opinion or in approach to the same medical condition based on that doctor's previous experience and training. It's so sad. For example, I became an orthopaedic surgeon because I like instant gratification. I like to fix things. If it's broken, I want to fix it. God has blessed me with a good set of hands, and I believe in my surgical specialty and my surgical skill set. That's why I became an orthopaedic surgeon. So if you're broken and you come to see me, I will fix you, often surgically. That's what I do. Now if you don't need surgery, don't get me wrong; I will treat you conservatively. But if you do, I'm not going to waste your time and mine by treating you nonoperatively when I know it's not going to help you. Well, there are other doctors who don't do this. Every patient just gets treated with physical therapy and medications like Motrin, Advil, Aleve, or ibuprofen for years and years, and the patient never really gets "fixed." I wonder to myself why that doctor even chose to be a surgeon, but who am I to judge? Again, just a different approach and a different opinion. Patients have every right to see other doctors and get other opinions. I just don't think physicians should be pummeled on social media or in online reviews for making their recommendations, that's all. Show some respect. Remember the doctor you just bashed online committed ten years of his or her life to formal education in this profession so that he or she could give back to and serve their community of patients. Have some respect and courtesy.

AUTONOMY

Fortunately, some form of autonomy still exists today, but much less so than it did in the past. At least for most, but not for all. Nowadays, more and more physicians are being employed by megagroups and large hospital systems. The days of solo, independent health care practitioners are virtually gone. Declining reimbursements and increases in overhead have made it almost cost-prohibitive to survive as an independent health care provider. Instead, doctors are partnering or joining large groups or hospital systems so that they gain more leverage in negotiating payer contracts with insurance companies. It's all about the concepts of strength in numbers and economies of scale. In the end, in these typical employment models, many doctors have lost the autonomy they enjoyed for so long as solo practitioners but, in exchange, were allowed to survive. So many of these seasoned physicians are now forced to answer the bureaucrats and suits who run these organizations. To them, however, it's a fair trade, allowing them to remain afloat. I'm sorry, but I could never do that. No way. No how. I'm old-school. That's not what I come from. That's not what I learned growing up. No defeat, baby, no surrender! Well, ladies and gentlemen, I'm happy to share with you that there is another way, and I look forward to sharing it with you. All you must do is keep reading.

REWARD

Regarding reward, nothing has changed. I would still argue today that medicine is the most rewarding profession that one could enjoy. This is especially true in fields such as orthopaedic surgery, which is the specialty that I am fortunate enough to call my own. In orthopaedics,

I satisfy my professional need for what I call instant gratification. As I mentioned earlier, when something's broken or torn, I fix it. Where there's pain, I erase it. Oh, you have arthritis? Well, don't be dismayed. It'll be gone in an hour or two after I perform a simple hip, knee, shoulder, or ankle replacement. Suddenly, the pain, swelling, redness, warmth, deformity, and limp are gone. Patients love you as you have restored their quality of life, and they are extremely grateful to you. Nothing is better. Nothing is more rewarding. Trust me.

What's so nice about orthopaedics, in general, is that you're usually dealing with a healthy, active population. We're typically not dealing with chronic diseases that must be managed forever. We can often fix our patients' problems permanently and erase their diseases off the map. Yes, that's right. We often cure them of their conditions—permanently. Talk about rewarding! So many other medical professions can only just manage their patients' chronic medical conditions and they do this for years and years—diseases that will never, *ever* be cured, but only managed with the continuation of medications and/or treatments. Not so in orthopaedics. What could be better than that? Nothing.

INCOME

Income, on the other hand, is not what it was. Doctors still do well—don't get me wrong—but not like we used to. Remember medical school is very expensive, and this is on top of the debt we already incurred during college, which as we all know is almost equally as expensive. Remember the average physician doesn't start his or her career until he or she is in their early thirties, and by that time, they're often between $200,000 and $500,000 in debt from school loans, depending on which undergraduate college and medical school he or she attended. According to the Medical Group Management Association (MGMA) Survey, the average physician salary in 1999 when I started was $150,000 per year for primary care physicians and around $250,000 annually for specialists. Now, according to the 2023 Medscape Physician Compensation Report, the average salary for primary care physicians ranges from $200,000 to $250,000 per year and between $300,000 to $550,000 per year for specialists, depending on their specialty. These numbers sound OK, but keep in mind that the average total school debt for graduating medical students is over $250,000. Furthermore, these incomes represent salaries of employed physicians and not the profits of the small business owners. For the physician small business owner who can't always afford to take a fixed salary but sometimes must live off the available cash flow of the business, these figures could represent gross income, not net income. Then when he or she accounts for ever-increasing annual overhead expenses, their net income figures shrink significantly.

To make matters worse, we used to get paid "fair market value" (FMV) for services rendered. It was a "fee-for-service" model. Now unfortunately, we get paid according to the payer's fee schedule. Believe it or not, the payers actually dictate to us the "value" of the service rendered by the health care provider. We don't even have a say. I mean can you believe that? Can you imagine going into a car dealership and saying, "I want that Cadillac Escalade, but I am only going to pay $20,000 for it"? Well, that's what's happening to us physicians. The value of our wisdom, knowledge, understanding, judgment, discernment, guidance, direction, and skill set that we're "selling" is being dictated to us by the insurance companies paying for our services. It's sort of backward, if you think about it, but it is what it is. Essentially, we have become slaves to the payers. If we choose to participate with these insurance companies (and most everyone does) and become one of their credentialed providers so that their customers (our patients) can have access to us, we can only accept what the insurance companies dictate is their "allowable amount" (amount they are willing to pay us) for the service provided. Yes, you read that correctly, and it's regardless of what we charge or what we think is fair and reasonable. Well, unfortunately, year after year, these "allowable amounts" continue to decrease, but at the same time, expenses continue to rise. You know how it is. Employees want an annual "cost of living" increase. The landlord wants more and more each year for the lease of his or her office space. Vendor supply costs continue to increase. Insurance premiums increase annually. Well, physician practices, for sure, are not immune to any of these escalations.

All of this would be fine, if all things were equal, but unfortunately, for us physicians, they're not. They're not because payers continue to decrease our reimbursement rates year over year. In other industries, when overhead goes up, they just raise the prices of the goods they are selling to make up the difference. During inflationary times in this country, traditional businesses just pass on costs of goods increases to customers. In those scenarios, only customers suffer. We can't do that in medicine. In our profession, we can raise our prices all we want, but that doesn't do anything, because the insurance companies would still dictate to us what they are going to pay. So in health care, only health care providers suffer. Without fail, insurance companies increase their annual premiums to the public while simultaneously paying the health care providers less year over year. Season after season, the payers become more profitable and the stability of the health care providers more precarious. It's a sinking ship, and many doctors have decided to bail to avoid drowning. Others have opted to join forces or to concede and become employed physicians just to wash their hands of this nonsense.

MEDICINE IS STILL THE GREATEST

Don't get me wrong. Medicine is still a highly sought-after field. It's still a very competitive profession and you still must be an exceptional candidate. Again, as stated previously, although there is still a great emphasis on earning an excellent GPA and MCAT score, it seems that, more recently, there has been an even greater emphasis on extracurricular activities and the "soft skills" of the applicants. And again, as mentioned, according to the AAMC, the average GPA for matriculants was 3.75 and the average MCAT score was 512 in 2022–2023, but many admission panels are focusing more and more on things such as research, leadership roles, and applicant participation in volunteer work as well.

So if your desire and passion is to be a physician, please go for it. If you're doing it for the right reasons, you will not be disappointed. Trust me. But the key is that you absolutely must, and I mean *must,* be sure that you're going into it for the right reasons, and with an innate desire to serve, because it will consume so much of you.

The purpose of this book is to not dissuade you from going into medicine. Quite the contrary. I truly want to encourage you to pursue this exceptional profession and to enjoy all the fruits that it has to offer. I want to help you prosper in every regard. Enjoy your prestigious occupation. Revel in your autonomy. Bask in your well-earned prosperity and relish the doctor-patient relationship that you have worked so hard to forge over the years. In my humble opinion, medicine is still the greatest and most prestigious profession in the world. There is nothing else I would rather do. It truly is such a privilege and blessing to be a physician and to have patients entrust us with their lives. There is no greater honor.

In this book, I'm going to tell you my story and how I accomplished everything. Unfortunately, as I have already mentioned, they don't teach us anything about the business of medicine in medical school. I guess they expect us to wing it and learn it on the fly as we're thrown in with the wolves. I'm going to tell you how I went from solo practice to small group practice to large joint venture with the largest health care institution in the state of New Jersey. These are my secrets for your success so that you can enjoy the honor and privileges of this career that you have been blessed with. "If at first you don't succeed, try, try again." Whatever you do, don't give up. I believe strongly that becoming a physician is a God-given gift. One that we should cherish and hold firmly. One that we should protect with all our heart. One that we should honor, revere, and respect.

CHAPTER 2

The Seven C's

To succeed as a physician, you must be a person of high moral integrity and possess certain innate values and ethics. Certain principles must compose your internal being. These characteristics must be weaved and woven into your DNA and must constitute your inner moral fiber. "What are these traits?" you ask. Well, they all fall into seven buckets that I call my Seven C's, and they are (in no particular order) character, conduct, conversation, compassion, care, conscientiousness, and commitment.

CHARACTER

Our character is who we are. What does our heart, mind, soul, and conscience say about us? Do we have grit? Are we trustworthy? Honorable? Principled? Honest? Reliable? Do we have the strength, courage, and resolve to make a difference for humanity? Do we live primarily for ourselves, or for others? Do we love our neighbors as ourselves? Do we put others before or after ourselves? Do we empathize with others that are hurting or in need, or do we care less? Do we give to charities or keep everything to ourselves? Do we have a heart for people? In Christian circles, we call these qualities the "fruits of the Spirit" and these fruits are love, joy, peace, patience, kindness, goodness, faithfulness, gentleness, and self-control. The Holy Bible tells us that once we put our trust in Jesus Christ as our Lord and Savior, our eternal security is sealed by the Holy Spirit and our bodies become the temple of the Holy Spirit of God who dwells within us. From that point forward, we are empowered to bear these fruits of the Spirit, which will enable us to be more Christlike in our character, conduct, and conversation with others. Indeed, all these Spiritual fruits and qualities apply here, and if you want to be the best doctor you can be, it would behoove you and all of us to bear these fruits of the Spirit in our character, conduct, and conversation, daily. Just imagine what health care would look like if every physician exuded these fruits each and every day. I can tell you this: the ones that do will prosper and flourish at an exponential growth rate.

CONDUCT

As they say, "Actions speak louder than words." How we conduct ourselves daily speaks volumes about our character. Do you behave in a way worthy of being called a physician and hanging up your shingle? Do you courteously hold the door for others, or do you walk right through? Do you say please and thank-you all the time? Do you write thank-you cards and emails when you should, or do you have to be reminded? Do you get back to people promptly? Are you kind, respectful, and courteous to everyone always? Do you treat everyone equally regardless of age, ethnicity, religion, race, gender, sexual orientation, and socioeconomic status? How do you speak to and treat your staff? Your patients? Are you professional at all times? How do you present yourself to others? Are you neat and tidy? Well-dressed? Presentable? Are you well-mannered with good etiquette? If not, you will fail. You either have what it takes, or you don't. It's either in you, or it's not. If it's not, I implore you to pursue another career. Medicine is not for you.

CONVERSATION

Patients need to be heard and respected. We cannot dictate to them. We need to be able to converse with them. Actually converse. That means it's a two-way street. Are you a good listener or just a good talker? You can't do all the talking when you're a doctor. You actually need to be a better listener than talker. As we all know, 90 percent of the time we can make a diagnosis, or at least a strong differential diagnosis, just by listening to our patients. So listen to them! Remember they know their own bodies much better than we ever could. We measure objectively. They measure subjectively. It's a big difference. So shut up and listen to them. It's not a conversation if we do all the talking. If I only had a dollar for every patient who told me that their first doctor "wouldn't let me talk—he wouldn't listen to a word I was saying and he just kept cutting me off," I would be a millionaire right now (ha ha ha). Patients want to be heard, and they also want to know that we actually heard and understood them. How do you speak to others? Are you thoughtful? Do you articulate well? Are your thoughts reasonable, logical, and rational? Are you composed? Can you organize your thoughts well and communicate them professionally and in an organized and structured manner that is easy to follow and understand? These are all requirements and necessary ingredients in the secret recipe for success in the business of medicine and for mastering the art of the doctor–patient relationship.

COMPASSION

Do you have a heart for people? Would others call you a kind and compassionate person? Do you love your neighbor as yourself? Do you have an innate desire to serve others and to help those that are hurting? Do you regularly give to charities to help the poor, hurting, less fortunate, and the suffering, or is that someone else's problem? Are you the first person to lend a hand, or the last? You can't be a successful physician if you don't care about people. This is not something you learn. This is something you're either born with or you're not. I mean we go into this profession, first and foremost, because we care about people and want to help them get better. We want to serve people because we love people. Again, going back to our reference to Christianity and now specifically, in Luke 10, one of the parables of Jesus, the question you need to ask yourself is this: would you be the first guy, the second guy, or the Good Samaritan? If the answer is the Good Samaritan, you can at least check off this box.

CARE

Do you truly care to be a physician? The Bible also teaches us that the Holy Spirit empowers believers with certain gifts of the Spirit. Not only fruits but gifts. Some of those gifts include leadership, prophecy, giving, exhortation, teaching, etc. Another one of those gifts is the gift of service, and another is mercy. Do you have the gift of service? Of mercy? Do you have a servant's heart? Does your heart bleed for people? Are you in it for the right reasons or for the wrong reasons? If you truly care, you will want to make a difference. You will want to help people get better and you will lose sleep over this until they do. When patients suffer, it truly affects you. It changes your mood and makes you sad. When they hurt, you hurt. When they cry, you cry. You will want to do everything in your power to help them and will jump through hoops for your patients to make them better. You will fight with insurance companies as you serve as their patient advocate. You will rearrange your schedule to accommodate them. You will add them on to your surgical schedule or clinic days because you care and want to get them out of pain as soon as possible, even if it's inconvenient for you to do so. You need to have a "never say no" mindset in practice. It must be your mantra and the modus operandi of your entire organization. This is how you know you're in it for the right reasons. This is how you know you care.

CONSCIENTIOUSNESS

To be successful in anything in life, you need to be extremely disciplined and conscientious. And being a physician is no different. In fact, it's probably even more important in this field than in any other given the fact that patients' lives are at stake. You need to keep your finger on the pulse of your patients and your practice twenty-four hours a day, seven days a week, 365 days a year. You can't miss anything. You need close follow-up with your patients. You cannot afford to lose them to follow-up. It could be a disaster if you miss something. Don't be cavalier. We're not God. We're not omniscient, omnipotent, or omnipresent like He is. Therefore, order studies and see patients back regularly to interpret their test results. Doing so gives you another opportunity to reassess the patient as well. Sometimes, this second look can be a lifesaver. The more times we interact with our patients, the more information we will garner, and the less likely it is that we will misdiagnose and/or mistreat them. Get more information. Remember to a physician, information is king. It's everything to a detective or private investigator, and it's everything to a doctor as well. The more information we have, the better the likelihood that we will make the right diagnosis, not miss things, and treat the patient properly. A breach in any of these areas could be a matter of life or death. A physician must maintain a mastery of wisdom, knowledge, understanding, judgment, truth, and discernment. There is no room for error. We must be thorough and meticulous. Period. There is no other way to succeed. Doing so speaks of your high level of conscientiousness.

COMMITMENT

To be a successful doctor, you must be fully committed to your practice, and that means fully committed to your patients. You can't neglect them. You must be available to them twenty-four hours a day, seven days a week, 365 days a year or, at a bare minimum, provide adequate coverage for them in your absence. Yes, I understand you need to have a personal life too, but we can't neglect our patients and must make ourselves available to them, even if it's through adequate coverage. Patients come first. It's a commitment we make to our patients and profession when we each swear that Hippocratic oath. This must always be honored and cherished. Look. This comes as no surprise to any of us going into this discipline. We know this. It comes with the territory. So don't even attempt to enter this field if you're not cut out for it or willing to make sacrifices for the betterment of your patients. Just don't. Please. For the sake of our patients, just don't. Just like the New York Giants were "all in," we must be "all in" as physicians caring for our vulnerable patients who have entrusted us with their care.

CHAPTER 3

Getting Started

OK, so you finally finished your rigorous training. I know. You thought this time would never come. After all the sleepless nights, shed tears, lost time, and endless effort you put into getting here, you're now ready to be rewarded. But what's next? What do you do? Then you quickly come to a realization. "Oh wow! Nobody ever taught me what to do next, or what to expect, or even how to plan for this!" We learn everything else in medical school and in our subsequent training—yes, everything we need to know clinically—but almost nothing regarding how to start, build, maintain, and grow a thriving medical practice. Everyone says the same thing when they get out of training. "Nobody ever taught me this stuff in my medical school, residency, or fellowship training." It's so sad. You spend all this time, money, and effort into becoming the best doctor you can be, but nobody teaches that medicine is a small business too. That's right. Medicine is a trade, after all. Just like being a plumber, a carpenter, or an electrician. It's a special trade, and to be successful, you must respect the fact that you have to run a successful business as well. You can't just be a great doctor. You must be a great businessman or businesswoman, too!

"So how do you do it?" Well, I'm so glad you asked, and now I'm going to tell you. But let me make it clear that it's not easy, but most things worth attaining rarely are. So here goes.

WORK HARD

First and foremost, you must work hard. It's just like anything else. Nothing is going to be handed to you on a silver platter. You must earn it. You must pay your dues. Well, in medicine, that means you must take a lot of emergency room calls at local hospitals. For the nonmedical reader, being "on call" is a privilege and opportunity to grow your practice by being the doctor the emergency room physicians call that day (or week) when a patient is in the emergency room in need of your services. As that doctor, he or she must make himself or herself available to answer phone calls or to make emergency in-person consultations almost immediately. That means he or she will most likely not be able to commit to any personal plans or commitments to friends or family like shows, movies, dinner reservations, etc. However, being the on-call doctor for a local emergency room is a great way to build your practice. In the beginning, no one knows you from Adam. As such, no one is going to support your practice by referring new patients to you until you prove yourself. So taking call and doing great work is a fantastic way to build your own patient following as well as a strong name and reputation. It's important to note that I said build your own name and reputation. Don't inherit someone else's. Earn it. Taking calls is your opportunity to shine. First impressions are everything. So make sure that you do everything right. Don't make patients wait. Introduce yourself. Be kind, compassionate and caring. Be nice. Smile. Make it such that when you walk away, the patient and their family members all comment to each other how much they like you and how confident they are in you. Listen to their complaints, the history of their present illness, then crush the focused physical exam, interpret the objective studies, and formulate a sound differential diagnosis and treatment plan. Knock it out of the park, and then make sure that they follow up with you. They must leave that local emergency room happy with you and the encounter they had with you.

First impressions are everything. As you're building your reputation and establishing yourself in your new community, make sure to only get credentialed at reputable hospitals and surgical centers with nothing less than stellar reputations. Make sure to avoid all those that don't possess such credentials and awards. Remember you're setting the bar for your patients' expectations. Remember what our moms always told us. "You are who your friends are!" Well, this pertains to our professional network as well. You are what and whom you associate yourself with. What you see is what you get. Trash in, trash out. Therefore, only associate yourself with the best of the best, and you will become part of that class very soon. That is, provided you deliver. And you must to succeed.

Every opportunity that we are blessed with to have patients entrust us with their medical care is an opportunity to build or destroy your name, reputation, brand, and practice. And I mean every opportunity. So don't blow it. Every single patient encounter is important, and we can never, ever, ever take any of them for granted. If you do, sooner rather than later your reputation will be destroyed as word-of-mouth reviews spread like wildfire. The second you start taking patients for granted, you are doomed. You must think like I do whereby every patient matters. I want a 100 percent success rate with every patient encounter and experience. Each of my patients matters so much to me. Their reviews of me as a health care practitioner, and of the practice, mean everything to me. I could receive one hundred five-star reviews, but if I get even one four-star or below review, my day is wrecked and I will lose sleep over it. Such reviews trigger immediate and full-blown service recovery, and it continues until every patient is fully satisfied. I recognized many years ago that I am in a service industry and to me, patient (customer) satisfaction is everything!

Next, make sure you have at least one late night of office hours each week. Success in business is all about meeting demand with supply. The fact of the matter is some patients just can't carve out time for themselves even to see a doctor. For them, work is just way too busy. So what's the antidote for this? Open night hours. Even if it's one day per week. Make sure you are available to accommodate this tranche of patients after they get out of work. If you don't, someone else will—like me.

Along these lines, I suggest that you work Saturdays, too. Nothing builds a practice faster than making yourself available to see patients on Saturdays. Remember health care is a service industry. Nothing shows better customer service than making yourself available on a Saturday. Talk about going above and beyond for your patients! Wow! Almost no one does this, but doing this was so critical to my success. It made me stand out from my competitors. This made it so convenient for my patients who didn't have the time to see a doctor during their busy work weeks. As an orthopaedic surgeon, I used my Saturday clinic hours to also offload the local emergency rooms. Patients soon learned that they could go right to me, the orthopaedic specialist, on a Saturday instead of killing a few hours in a local hospital's emergency room. Suddenly, these patients had immediate access to the specialist. It was virtually unheard of, especially in my field of orthopaedic surgery. I did this for years when my kids were younger, when they couldn't even realize I was gone. My kids would sleep in on Saturdays and by the time they woke up around 11 a.m. (I know, 11 a.m.!), I had already seen about thirty patients. I started rather early on Saturday mornings. It was a relaxed and casual dress-down day in clinic. It was great. Patients would come in. Lots of them would bring coffee, bagels, and doughnuts. It was awesome for business but even better for forging strong, healthy, long-lasting, personal doctor-patient relationships. Before I knew it, my Saturday morning hours from 8 a.m. to 12 p.m. turned into almost a full day from 8 a.m. to 3 or 4 p.m. When my kids got older and started to participate in sports, they became my number one priority. As such, I killed the Saturday hours thing, but my practice was already booming, and I didn't need to do that anymore. Now my junior physicians maintain Saturday hours because it's great for business and developing their own doctor-patient relationships, and the torch has been passed.

The point is to do what you have to do to establish an outstanding, top-shelf reputation early on in your practice. Once that reputation is developed, it will follow you for the rest of your career. Don't forget this advice.

ESTABLISH A NICHE, AND KNOW YOUR MARKET

Before you hang up your shingle, I strongly recommend that you first know your market. You need to first identify if there is even a need for you and your expertise in this proposed catchment area. Is the area already oversaturated with physicians who possess your skill set? You can find this out by simply doing a Google search for physicians in your specialty near you. You can also speak to local residents and physicians in the area. Finally, you can consider calling your health insurance company and inquire that way as well. If the area is already inundated with competition, choose another location. Why would you want to go up against headwinds when you could have the wind at your back instead? Just like in real estate, it's all about location, location, location. And again, in the business of medicine, it's all about supply and demand. You must do your due diligence before committing to an area. It's a big deal to start, or even join, a practice, and you should not make this decision lightly.

If you identify that there is, in fact, a need for your expertise, your next step then is to distinguish yourself from others. There must be a reason why patients should choose you over others. What makes you different? Why should patients go to you instead of to another physician? Do you have unique training? Do you have a specialty? Are your results and outcomes much better than your competitors? Are you the only one doing this procedure or offering this special service? Did you pioneer any specific cutting-edge technology? Are you the local expert with the most experience in a certain area? What is it? If you want to stand out among the crowd of competition, find out what your niche is.

For me, I always took pride in promoting state-of-the-art orthopaedic technologies in the New York and New Jersey Tristate area. At Kayal Orthopaedic Center, we are and have always been ahead of the curve when it comes to the implementation of advanced orthopaedic technologies and procedures. Some of these advancements that we have helped pioneer include, but are not limited to, the usage of computer-assisted navigation technologies in the areas of hip and knee replacement surgeries, the utilization of gender-specific, high-flexion, female-gender total knee replacement surgery, the use of MRI-based, patient-specific, customized, partial, and total knee replacement surgeries, outpatient partial and total joint replacement surgeries, minimally invasive orthopaedic surgeries, robotic-assisted partial and total joint replacement surgeries, hip preservation surgeries, usage of orthopaedic biological regenerative medicine therapies such as platelet rich plasma, anterior cruciate ligament repair surgeries, and most recently, minimally invasive endoscopic spine surgeries performed through seven-millimeter incisions, just to name a few. Year after year, our surgeons are awarded the highest and most coveted kudos and accolades in the field for their surgical expertise and medical advancements.

As a regional pioneer of many of these procedures and others, many new patients continue to come through our doors requesting these technologies, and specifically me as their surgeon, as word spreads like wildfire in and about our communities. I must say it's a great feeling as it provides tangible and palpable feedback as fulfillment of my dreams and aspirations.

Well, needless to say, this helped me to build a very successful orthopaedic practice rather quickly.

And one final thought. Regarding this new office of yours, please make sure it's beautiful, comfortable, inviting, and state-of-the art. Again, everything and everyone you employ is a reflection of you as a physician. Medicine is a clean and sterile field. Patients expect and deserve this when they come to you. No one wants to walk into an old, filthy, decrepit office. As such, make sure it's clean, modern, and presentable. If you can't do it now, renovate it as soon as you can. Doing so will lead to a great return on your investment. You have my word.

HAVE A DIVERSIFIED PORTFOLIO

Simply put, take all insurances. As a health care provider who has been blessed with the gift, honor, and privilege of becoming a physician, you should not be fussy and only cherry-pick the best insured patients. When you first hang up your shingle, and for the rest of your career for that matter, you should consider it an honor and privilege that even one patient is calling to see you. We must never take for granted that patients actually choose to see us. They can go anywhere, but they choose us. When they do, I feel honored and privileged. So should you. Even today, I see all patients from all payers that I am credentialed with.

From a business perspective, and like in wealth management investment strategies, it's also good to ensure you're not putting all your eggs into one basket. Make sure that you have and maintain a well-diversified portfolio. So, for instance, at Kayal Orthopaedic Center, we participate in Medicare, commercial insurance plans, handle personal injury cases, workman's compensation cases, and care for the uninsured, cash-paying population as well. This way, like in the market, if one payer area gets hit hard one year, or if legislation changes, there are other revenue streams that would still allow for adequate cash flow to survive and keep the lights on. At Kayal Orthopaedic Center, we maintain a well-diversified portfolio of insurance company participation allowing us to see virtually every patient desiring our services.

I have seen many practices fail over the years because they have violated this principle. Unfortunately, with all their eggs in one basket, when the personal injury feeder's or workman's compensation's case manager's hand got "cut off," the practice got killed and crashed soon thereafter.

Heed the warning.

NETWORK

The key to success in most businesses is relationships. It's not any different in the field of medicine. Get your name out there. Introduce yourself to local referral sources, which can include other primary care physicians, emergency room doctors, urgent care facilities, chiropractors, physical therapists, athletic trainers, coaches, personal injury attorneys, workman's compensation case managers, and others, for example. Give out your contact information, especially your cell phone number, and tell everyone that you can see their referrals for same-day appointments, twenty-four hours a day, seven days a week, 365 days a year. The only problem with this approach, however, is that relationships can sometimes change on a dime. So what that means is that you can lose these referral sources at any time, even without prior notice. It's tough to start these relationships, but it's even harder to maintain them. So work them. It takes a lot of concierge-like customer service, and nothing short of continued excellence in medical care, but it's certainly worth the effort.

As good as these relationships are, however, nothing is better than the establishment and maintenance of a solid, excellent, and strong reputation in medicine that will stick with you throughout your career. And, as we all know, nothing demonstrates this better than the coveted warm-market referral from a prior patient or their family members. That said, referrals from your professional network of friends and colleagues are a close second. It's just a fact of life that people like to refer to their friends. It's called networking. It's friends referring to friends, referring to friends, and so on and so forth. It's what makes the world go round. Like they say, "It's not what you know. It's who you know." Others say that more deals are made on golf courses than anywhere else in the world. Others claim that a third of golfers are doing business on the golf course. Why should medicine be any different? There's nothing wrong with networking in medicine, provided you are always doing what's best for your patients and not referring to these providers because of what's expected in return, if you know what I mean. No kickbacks. You must not violate any regulatory issues pertaining to referrals. Everything must pass the smell test and be at arm's length. Always put the patient first. Never compromise on this principle. So if you need to refer to another physician, why not refer to a friend you know and trust? A friend who has cared for other patients of yours in the past, all of whom have enjoyed excellent outcomes. This colleague, because of your relationship, will often ultimately care for your referral like "family" and go the extra mile for your patient––first, because of your friendship, and––second, to further impress you with the hope to gain even more referrals in the future.

The prerequisite, however, is that you ensure that you must only encircle yourself around the crème de la crème in your network of medical experts. Remember what we said before? You are what and who your friends are. The best hospitals, the best doctors, and the best network of referral sources. Only those with the best reputations, because, as we've said a million times, reputations mean everything to us and to our patients. This is the art of the deal that you must master. You must *ace* this. Again, only the best for the best. If you want to be the best, you must surround yourself with the best. Don't ever forget that your referrals are a reflection of you.

Keep in mind, however, that your referral sources will stop sending to you, regardless of how much they may love you, if your patients and clients don't have great personal experiences with you, your office, and your staff. Yes, even your staff. Every interaction leaves an impression. Our staff can make or break our practice. Your outcomes and reviews to the referral source must be excellent. The feedback to your network of referral sources has to be overwhelmingly positive for these referrals to continue. If it is not, this referral source (and its associated revenue stream) will very quickly die on the vine.

Do your best to have a strong networking group. If we're all in this together, working in earnest to care for our mutual community of patients, we may as well be doing this with our friends. After all, we're all in it for the same reasons.

Hopefully.

CHAPTER 4

You Must Be Great

I know it sounds arrogant, but I must say it's true. It's not good enough to be a good doctor. You must be a great doctor. Good doctors can do OK, but the truth is they often struggle. Think about your colleagues right now. I'm sure you can think of many very good doctors out there who are failing. They are good physicians, surgeons, chiropractors, podiatrists, and therapists, but they're failing. They are busy, their practices are booming, but they are just getting by or actually losing money each year. They struggle to succeed, to make a profit, to meet payroll, to compete with their peers, to retain staff, to retain patients, to manage overhead, to remain current in their fields, to balance their personal and professional lives, and/ or they struggle by having to defend recurrent malpractice claims coming from disgruntled and poorly managed patients. In essence, they struggle to flourish and to thrive. That's probably why you're interested in reading this book in the first place. You're probably able to relate to at least one of these issues right now and you're just so tired of this struggle.

Well, there is hope. Just continue reading.

Medicine is tough. It's tough on our minds, our brains, and our bodies. It stresses every aspect of our lives. It takes us away from our friends, our family, other pleasures, and even ourselves. It just consumes us. Our patients are always on our minds. Running the practice is always on our minds. Paying our bills is always on our minds. Meeting payroll is always on our minds. As such, you're probably looking for some serious help. "How can I do this better and more efficiently?" you ask. "How can I become more profitable? How can I better develop my practice, name, and reputation?" Well, this book is going to help you to answer these questions and others by mastering the business of medicine and the doctor-patient relationship. But to do so, you must become a great doctor. If you want a stellar reputation, you must be great. If you want excellent outcomes, you must be great. If you desire a happy patient population, as opposed to one that is angry, bitter, frustrated, and disgruntled, patients must consider you to be a great doctor. Period. There is no way around it. Your ratings and your reviews must be five-star. Not four-star. Four-star doctors do OK. Five-star doctors are great and can take it to the next level. You must be a doctor who receives all the highly esteemed and coveted awards in medicine: Castle-Connolly, Top Doctor, SRC Master surgeon, SRC Center of Excellence, Vitals Compassionate-Doctor, Vitals Patients'-Choice, etc.—not just once but year after year. The word on the street about you must be top-notch. Patients must love you. If they do, word will spread like wildfire and you will be great! Trust me.

You see, excellent health care is everyone's number one priority. Patients don't compromise on this. You wouldn't, I wouldn't, so why would we expect our patients to? Patients have choices. As such, you must make them want to choose you. When they can choose between a good doctor and a great doctor, they will always choose the great doctor.

Remember there are great and horrible tradespeople in every craft. There are great and horrible plumbers, electricians, and carpenters. Well, doctors are not immune to this. There are great and horrible physicians, too. Just remember you must be one of the great ones.

Great physicians also honor the Hippocratic oath. Just to refresh your memory, in its classic form, it says,

> I swear by Apollo Healer, by Asclepius, by Hygieia, by Panacea, and by all the gods and goddesses, making them my witnesses, that I will carry out, according to my ability and judgment, this oath and this indenture.
>
> To hold my teacher in this art equal to my own parents; to make him partner in my livelihood; when he is in need of money to share mine with him; to consider his family as my own brothers, and to teach them this art, if they want to learn it, without fee or indenture; to impart precept, oral instruction, and all other instruction to my own sons, the sons of my teacher, and to indentured pupils who have taken the Healer's oath, but to nobody else.
>
> I will use those dietary regimens which will benefit my patients according to my greatest ability and judgment, and I will do no harm or injustice to them. Neither will I administer a poison to anybody when asked to do so, nor will I suggest such a course. Similarly, I will not give to a woman a pessary to

cause abortion. But I will keep pure and holy both my life and my art. I will not use the knife, not even, verily, on sufferers from stone, but I will give place to such as are craftsmen therein.

Into whatsoever houses I enter, I will enter to help the sick, and I will abstain from all intentional wrong-doing and harm, especially from abusing the bodies of man or woman, bond or free. And whatsoever I shall see or hear in the course of my profession, as well as outside my profession in my intercourse with men, if it be what should not be published abroad, I will never divulge, holding such things to be holy secrets.

Now if I carry out this oath, and break it not, may I gain for ever reputation among all men for my life and for my art; but if I break it and forswear myself, may the opposite befall me.

Great doctors "primum non nocere." Great doctors first do no harm to their patients.

To be a great doctor, you must have great outcomes. If you do, your patients' word-of-mouth recommendations for your services will quickly disseminate. Online reviews are huge now. People check everything these days. They check movie reviews, restaurant reviews, travel destination reviews, and certainly, because it pertains to their health, the reviews of their physicians and surgeons. So make sure they're great and that you're considered a five-star great physician.

To be a great physician, you must be the quarterback of their care. You must own the doctor-patient relationship. You must stay in control. Yes, listen to your patients and have them participate in their care, but you are the one in charge of the patient encounter. Remember patients are coming to see you for your wisdom, knowledge, judgment, discernment, expertise, guidance, and direction. When I say take control, I mean take control. You must always keep your finger on the pulse. You must stay on top of your patient's medical condition and not miss anything. Care enough to be conscientious, thorough, and meticulous. Ensure close follow-up so that nothing, and I mean *nothing,* gets missed. And for heaven's sake, if a patient makes an appointment to see you, do something for them. They made the appointment for a reason, so help them! Do something to make them better! Don't be cavalier. Order studies. Order labs. Give them an injection! Do something!

Remember information is king. Whether it's the writing of a simple prescription for medicine or physical therapy, the administration of a cortisone injection, or ordering blood work, labs, an MRI, or EKG, do something. Otherwise, they're going to feel that they wasted their time coming to see you, and they will never come back to you or recommend you to others. Even worse, you may end up missing something, like a tumor or a cancer, God forbid. You must do something to help them and then see them back soon in follow-up. Even if you think not much is going on, remember they made the appointment for a reason. They came to see you to get treatment for their condition, so treat them. Remember they know their bodies way better than we ever could. So trust their instinct. Ordering something, even if it's just physical therapy, for instance, gives you an opportunity to see them back in a week or two just to see and examine them again. This will then afford you not only the opportunity to review any labs or studies that you ordered on the last visit, but also the ability to reassess their condition, listen to them, and perform another follow-up physical examination, just to make sure that nothing gets missed. Remember they came to you for a problem. It's our job to find it. So find it!

To become a great doctor, you also must stay current in your knowledge and skill set. You can't be left in the dust. You can't allow yourself to become an old, antiquated health care provider. Medical technologies continue to advance rapidly. The onus is on us to keep up. If we don't, we'll fall behind very quickly and lose patients to our competition. We owe it to ourselves and to our patients to do so. We must deliver for our patients. They deserve the best, and it's our job to oblige. You can't be the best unless you offer your patients the latest and greatest, state-of-the-art, cutting-edge technologies. If you don't, you're short-changing your patients, and that's not fair to them. It would be better for your patients for you to then refer them out to other great physicians, as opposed to keeping them in your practice. You owe it to our patients to do so, if you don't or won't offer those technologies yourselves. Remember with the advent of the internet, patients are becoming more and more educated. Most of the time, they already know what innovations are out there. They talk to their friends. They read about them in magazines and newspapers and online. They see the same ads, billboards, social media posts, and commercials that we do. You're a doctor. You want to be the best doctor for your patients. You want to be a great doctor for your patients. So stay current and up-to-date.

Some ways you can stay current are through continuing medical education (CME) credits. I, for instance, attend the American Academy of Orthopaedic Surgeons conference just about every year.

It's fabulous. Fortunately, to maintain your active licensure, CMEs are mandatory for most physicians already. If you're a surgeon, I strongly encourage you to take regular master surgeon courses and participate in cadaver labs regularly. I do. You should too.

CHAPTER 5

Brand Yourself

I f you're trying to master the business of medicine and grow your practice, you must advertise. There is no way around it. Why do you think staple brands such as Coca-Cola, Apple, and Microsoft still advertise? It must work! The problem is it's very expensive, especially when you do it properly. And what I mean by that is don't try to manage your marketing campaigns by yourself. You must hire a professional company that can properly brand your practice.

COMPANY NAME

It first starts with establishing a company name. It can't be too complicated or too long and should communicate something about your practice. Mine is simple: Kayal Orthopaedic Center. *Kayal,* because it's my last name, of course. *Orthopaedic* because the field of orthopaedics has always been my primary service line. *Center* because the practice is not just a traditional doctor's office; it's a whole center. We are a large, multispecialty, multidisciplinary, comprehensive musculoskeletal medical institution. We have over twenty office locations in New Jersey and New York. We offer the following services: general orthopaedic surgery, the treatment of spinal disorders, sports medicine and arthroscopy, MAKO robotic-assisted partial and total joint replacement surgery, hand, shoulder and upper extremity expertise, hip and knee surgeon experts, foot and ankle surgery expertise, fracture care, podiatry, the diagnosis and management of disorders of bone metabolism, osteoporosis, the diagnosis and treatment of rheumatological disorders, interventional pain management, physiatry, nonoperative orthopaedic medicine, physical therapy, chiropractic, acupuncture, massage therapy, IV infusion center, high-resolution cross-sectional medical imaging via MRI and CT scanning, DXA bone density testing, EMG and nerve conduction studies, digital x-ray technologies, ultrasound imaging, duplex ultrasound to evaluate for DVT, C-arm fluoroscopy for diagnosis and interventional treatments in surgical procedure rooms, and more! That's why we're a center.

As such, when you offer all of this, you want to tell the community about it. I mean who wouldn't want to go to a place where they can get everything taken care of at the same place? How great is it to not have to be referred out to another doctor or another practice? So our motto is this:

> Insist on excellence! Insist on Kayal Orthopaedic Center! Your one-stop-shop for all of your orthopaedic needs!

And trust me: we let people know.

COMPANY'S UNIFORM RESOURCE LOCATOR (URL)

So now that you have your company name, you need to develop a web site and logo. The web site should not be long. It should be as short as possible so that people can remember it. When I was first starting out in practice, I recall that I wanted my web site to be www. kayalorthopaediccenter.com. My marketing guy, Dan Antonelli from KickCharge, told me that the uniform resource locator, also known as the URL, was too long. Well, naturally, I was upset at first, but I soon realized that he was right. He convinced me to shorten it, and he recommended that I make it www.kayalortho.com. Well, thank God he did, and I'm still using the same URL all these years later. It's so much easier for patients to remember, and half of them would have spelled orthopaedic without the *a* and would have likely typed in the web site incorrectly. That's why it's important to pay the experts to be the experts. You get what you pay for. And besides, we should also stay in our lanes.

COMPANY'S WEB SITE

Now once you have the domain name and web site URL, make sure you have professional graphic designers create the web site. Remember it has to look great! Not good. Great. It must be professional. It, like everything else, is a reflection of you and your brand. As such, you want it to be great! Besides, there is so much that goes into creating a web site. It's not just the look. There are other things that not only enhance your patient's experience but also greatly improve your search engine optimization (SEO) that ultimately results in greater organic rankings on search engines like Google, Bing, Yahoo, and DuckDuckGo.

COMPANY'S LOGO

Well, now that you have your business name, domain, and web site, it's time for a logo. Logos are key. They are so instrumental in creating a successful brand. The colors, size, and shape all have to be right. The logo needs to represent well. It, too, has to be professional and of high-resolution. Again, pay professionals for their expertise. This is where Dan Antonelli and KickCharge come back into play. When I was rebranding the Kayal Orthopaedic Center many years ago, I asked him to keep the red and black colors in my original logo (made by another graphic designer) because I liked the colors together. I thought they looked cool. Well, Dan refused to oblige. I remember his words exactly. He said, "Rob, I'm not doing that. You can't do that. Your patients are going to see the logo and say, 'Great. You go to the Kayal Orthopaedic Center first to bleed (red) and then to die (black.)'" Well, needless to say, that's all I needed to hear! I quickly changed the colors of the logo to a cooler combination of blue, white, and titanium gray and haven't looked back since.

MARKET YOUR PRACTICE

Look. In this day and age, it's so important to market your practice. This can be done in a myriad of different ways. Traditionally, print ads in newspapers and magazines were the way to go. Now as we live in the digital age, these are becoming more and more obsolete. TV and radio commercials and billboards are great, of course, but we all know that they're also quite expensive. These days, your money is often best spent in the digital space. With digital, you probably get the best bang for your buck and return on investment (ROI). Everyone is always on the internet and on their phones and other devices. You know it, and I know it. So you may as well use it to your advantage.

Market your practice using Google Adwords and on social media platforms, such as Facebook, Instagram, LinkedIn, TikTok, and Twitter. Again, it's always best to do so professionally by letting the experts handle these campaigns so that your brand is properly maintained and communicated. I use the same teams for my web site design, content, hosting, graphic designs, logos, print ads, press releases, brochures, billboards, and almost everything else about creating, maintaining, and marketing my brand. They know everything about the practice and our product. After all, they helped me create the brand and they help me market it as well. Kayal Orthopaedic Center has become a staple household name in the New York and New Jersey Tristate area because of our consistency in marketing and branding of the practice year after year.

If finances restrain you, you can also market your practice for little to nothing by doing seminars in local VFW halls or community centers, by walking door to door in your community while introducing yourself to potential referral sources, and even by doing podcasts and posting them for free on YouTube. If you would like to view the *kayalortho* podcast that I created and maintain on YouTube, please feel free to check it out by searching "kayalortho podcast" on YouTube. Or if you're reading the digital form of this book, you can watch the podcast by clicking on the following link: https://www.youtube.com/playlist?list=PLEVHuYmRCVAgaG8En xOo3xvEyfkg-JqOe.

Regardless of how you view it, please make sure to *click* the notification button and *subscribe* to our Kayal Orthopaedic Center page on YouTube! Ha ha ha, I couldn't miss that opportunity!

Somehow you need to get the message out and do whatever it takes. You need to be innovative and always think outside the box. But you need to do it. Just do it. Remember if you don't, someone else, like me, will.

One last thing about advertising. You mustn't falsely advertise. No bait and switch tactics. You must deliver on your promises and on your marketing statements. That said, if you got it, there is nothing wrong with flaunting it. You worked for it. You put in the hours, and you earned it. So go for it. You may as well let the community know. After all, they deserve to know. They deserve the best that medicine has to offer. You can't worry about what your competition might feel. Instead, worry about the patients in the community and make sure they're aware of the latest and greatest technologies that are available to them.

CHAPTER 6

It's All about Customer Service

Medicine is a service industry. Because it's a service we provide to our local community, it essentially falls into the category of community service. But to excel in the business of medicine and to master the doctor-patient relationship, it must be a "white glove community service, Ritz-Carlton style." Nothing less.

"So what does that entail?" you ask.

NEVER SAY NO

Well, first and foremost, the entire practice, and all of its employees, must live by the mantra "Never say no" to any patient. We must accommodate them and their requests. Somehow. Some way. Just make it happen. "We aim to please" must be the mentality and mindset of the practice. It's OK for patients to cancel. It's OK that they're twenty-five minutes late for their appointment; we'll still see them. It's OK for them to reschedule. It's OK that they need to be seen *today*. It's OK that they just walked in when we were about to close in ten minutes. It's OK. The patients are always right. When your schedule is full, still add them if they want to be seen. Just remember to tell them that there may be a wait. Given that you're going out of your way for them, they're unlikely to care. When patients call, give them same-day appointments, or the next day at the very least. Don't make them wait days or weeks for an appointment, unless that is what they specifically request. If you do, you may lose them. We don't like to wait for things. Well guess what. Neither do our patients, especially when they're in pain.

SOLICIT FEEDBACK

It's important to have a suggestion box in all your waiting rooms. We need to actively solicit feedback from our patients on their way in and on their way out of our office. We need to find out what we could do better next time to enhance their experience at our medical practice. In fact, at our facilities, I call it the "Kayal Orthopaedic Center Experience." It's truly an experience, and one that I hope our patients will never forget. I believe that patients should be treated like gold during the entire circle of care, just like how we'd want our own family members to be treated. From the moment they call the office and the first person they greet to their exit to their vehicles, and every employee they've encountered every step in between, I want it to be an experience that they'll never forget. I want them to leave our facilities and say, "Wow! I've never experienced anything like this in any medical office ever before." Then on the way out, make sure you ask them if everything was OK with today's visit and if there's anything you or your staff could do better next time to make their experience more pleasurable. This will most certainly send a message to your patients that you care about their satisfaction and are willing to be open to constructive criticism to make the experience even better next time.

BE KIND AND COURTEOUS TO EVERY SINGLE PATIENT

I've always said that the physicians' call center staff and front desk staff could either make or break their practice. It doesn't take a rocket scientist or a brain surgeon to realize that these people create the patient's first impression to our practice. And as we all know, first impressions mean everything to people. Therefore, I always want our patients greeted kindly and with a smile. Even when we're talking to them on the phone. The smile will transmit right through the phone lines and directly to our patients' hearts and minds. And when you speak to them, I don't like patients being called by their first name. I just don't. It's a pet peeve of mine. I'm sorry, but I'm old-school. I don't do it, and I don't want my staff to do it. To me, it's rude and disrespectful. I'm all about proper etiquette. For me, it's "Mr. [or Mrs.] So and So." Or it's "sir" or "ma'am". And if they correct me (and they always do), I still do it. It's just the way I was raised, I guess. I don't care that I'm the doctor and they're the patient. To me, it's a respect thing, so be respectful. Plain and simple. Also, smile when you greet them. Make eye contact. Shake their hand. Don't interrupt them when they're speaking. Make sure they are appropriately covered during their physical examination. Ask them if they would feel more comfortable if a chaperone was also present during the encounter. All of this speaks volumes about your character, integrity, and level of professionalism. It also helps to build your name, reputation, and brand.

ANSWER THE PHONE *NOW*

I know that I am not alone when I say, "I hate when the phone rings and rings and rings and no one picks it up!" Well, it's no surprise that our patients do as well. Excellence in customer service demands that we answer the phones immediately, preferably on the first ring, but by the third at the latest. And when you answer the phone, always, always, always say, "Hello. You have reached the Kayal Orthopaedic Center. This is Kelly. How can I help you?" By doing so, you have

- confirmed that they called the correct place
- introduced yourself to the patient (so now they know who they're speaking to)
- provided service by a human instead of via an automated attendant
- avoided the universally despised voice mail service
- offered to help them, which is *exactly* what they need

If you let the phones ring and ring and ring and never pick them up or allow them to go to voicemail, you may as well remove that patient from your medical record database. He or she will find another doctor. Nobody wants or deserves such horrible service when they're calling *you* to give *you* business! The second that you start taking your patients for granted and think that they're irreplaceable, you're done.

RETURN PATIENTS' CALLS PROMPTLY

Please don't forget the business that we're in. Patients need us. They have questions and concerns. The world of medicine is foreign to most of them. That's why they so heavily rely on our guidance and direction. We can't neglect them. They often don't know what to expect with this condition or that one. Is this a normal side effect from that medication? Is this redness, warmth, or swelling normal after this surgery? They often have no clue what to do or what to expect with their condition, injury, medication, surgical scar, swelling, etc. So be there for them. Help them. Hold their hands. It will pay dividends in building an incredible medical practice, but an even better doctor-patient relationship. We're so privileged to have such a strong fund of knowledge in so many areas of medicine that we often forget how ignorant most of the general population is regarding the same. We need to be more empathetic and compassionate in this area, and if you are, I promise you your practice will thrive.

RESPECT PATIENTS' TIME

Time is money. Not just for us but for our patients as well. We must respect this phenomenon. Furthermore, we can *never* get time back. Once it's gone, it's gone. Who knows what else our patient had planned for the day? He or she could have had to catch a flight later in the day. Maybe another doctor's appointment? Perhaps it's their daughter's birthday? Who knows? What I do know, however, is that our patients' time is just as valuable as ours, and we must honor this. As such, I always try to stay on time. Most of the time, I do, but sometimes I don't. When I don't, as a courtesy to my patients, it's incumbent upon me and my staff to communicate that I'm behind and to make sure that our patients are OK with that. It's just the right thing to do. It's common courtesy. It's proper etiquette. It helps to communicate to our patients that we are sorry for running behind and that we respect their time as much as our own. Don't ever forget that they are choosing to come to us. We're not choosing them. Thus, the onus is on us to serve and to satisfy. Not the other way around.

HIRE THE RIGHT STAFF

It's so important when you run a business, especially one that is in the service industry, that you hire the right staff. As I've said over and over again, everyone who gets hired at Kayal Orthopaedic Center is a reflection of me and my standards. Everything trickles down from the top. The buck always stops with me. I am the one who's ultimately responsible for everything. So rest assured that my employees know that I feel this way and that they must represent the brand and level of excellence in health care that I have worked so hard to establish and maintain over the past twenty-five years. They must feel that pressure. I'm sorry, but I'm not going to risk compromising that for anything or anyone. So with over twenty locations and over 350 employees, it's clearly hard to ensure this all by myself. That's why I have an unbelievably stellar and professional group of administrators, directors, managers, and supervisors who lead by example, report to me regularly, and help execute and implement the modus operandi of the practice that I insist upon.

Regarding your employees, you can't be cheap. Remember you get what you pay for. Therefore, to retain them, you must at least offer a "fair market value" (FMV) or "the going rate" to your employees and a total compensation package that includes health benefits, vision, dental, and 401(k) pension plan and competes with the local hospitals.

Furthermore, always ensure that you are adequately staffed to keep your patients happy and to provide the caliber of service previously described. On this note, however, you must make sure you don't overstaff. If you do, the practice will quickly drown. Today, payroll makes up the lion's share of overhead for most businesses, so run your practice as a "lean green fighting machine." To do this, I'm always trimming the branches, pruning the shrubs, cleaning house, throwing out the trash, weeding the beds, or however you want to say it. I think you know what I mean. I run a tight ship. I like to always fire on all cylinders, and I ensure that we do. If you are of this mindset, you will last with me. If you are not, you won't. I always hold up my end of the deal. I expect the same from my employees, and I will not allow myself to be taken advantage of. I'm great to my staff. I expect the same reciprocity.

TAKE CARE OF YOUR PEOPLE

It's so important to take care of your employees. Don't abuse them. Pay them well, and reward them for their loyalty, commitment, and dedication to you and your practice. Although the patients are coming to see you, remember your staff can make or break your practice and reputation. So take care of them. In life, and in business, everyone needs and deserves to be happy. It cannot be a one-way street. This philosophy and understanding have paid dividends for me repeatedly in my practice. Simply put, it must be a win–win for everyone involved for relationships in business to last. Whether I'm acquiring a medical practice, signing on a physician or other health care professional, or hiring an office administrator or support staff, the thought process is the same for me: take care of them, and they'll take care of me and the practice. Treat them well, and they'll put their heart and soul into serving the practice. Treat them like I'd want my own family to be treated. Because of this mentality, the attrition rate at Kayal Orthopaedic Center always has been exceptionally low, especially for health care providers. Our practitioners just don't leave. Why? Because I'm great to them. I take care of them, and they take care of me and the practice in return. They work hard, but they get paid very well for their services. I do *not* abuse them. I ensure that they get their paychecks, bonuses, and raises as promised. They regularly get recognized, publicly and via employee-wide emails, with kudos and accolades. In addition, they always have my unwavering support, my utmost respect, and get to maintain and enjoy their autonomy as well. Who wouldn't want that from their employer? It truly is a fantastic place to work, I must say. Not only for the health care providers but for the staff, too. I have always considered Kayal Orthopaedic Center a home away from home for me and for all of us. It is our work family; it has always been and will always be that way. Way back when, when I only had five employees, we were so close with one another and treated each other like family. Now even with our 350 employees, although we don't see each other so frequently because of our size and multiple locations, they all still know that I'm only a visit, call, text, or email away from them and still available to each of them at their beck and call. They also know that my door is still always open to each one of them for not only work issues but for personal concerns as well. Why? Because I love my employees and care so much for them all. Every day, they choose to work at Kayal Orthopaedic Center, and that means so much to me. As such, if I can help them, I will. They're all so good to me and our patients, so the least I can do for them is to be there for them when in need.

HAVE MULTIPLE LOCATIONS

Here we go again about supply and demand. If the demand is there and you want to grow your empire, you need to be able to supply the service. However, we must always remember to be strategic in choosing our next location. Remember what they say about real estate? It's always about location, location, location. Make sure your next location captures a patient population that you're not currently serving. For me, I slowly grew the Kayal Orthopaedic Center footprint all over northern New Jersey and New York by strategically choosing locations that served a market I needed to tap into. This strategy has allowed me to scale this business successfully over and over again. For one reason or another, I wanted to be in certain markets. There were hospitals I wanted to support. There were opportunities that presented themselves. There were needs that needed to be met. There were referral sources I couldn't tap into unless I opened up shop there. By the grace of God, over and over and over again, every decision turned to gold because the moves were very strategic in nature. Furthermore, extensive due diligence was first performed, and each option was thoroughly vetted and contemplated before I pulled the trigger. Well, all thanks and praise be to God, each decision was better than the previous, and each return on investment (ROI) was greater than the one before.

MASTER SERVICE RECOVERY

Now because medicine is not a perfect science, sometimes—rarely— things can go wrong. People are human and humans aren't perfect. Neither are robots or computers, by the way. That being said, sometimes the errors are iatrogenic in nature (meaning that they were caused by mistakes made by the health care provider), and sometimes the patients themselves cause problems by being noncompliant with the doctor's orders or just by being high-risk patients. You see, there are also risk factors out of our control that increase patients' risks for complications. Some of these include, but are not limited to, obesity, smoking, diabetes, steroid usage, autoimmune diseases, lack of exercise, and other medical comorbidities.

Regardless of who's at fault, however, we as physicians are very sorry when patients experience a less than optimal outcome in their care. In fact, we're very, very, very sorry. Let me kick it up a notch. In reality, we're devastated. I personally lose sleep over these things. If a patient's outcome is less than perfect, I'm genuinely sad. I feel like a failure. It's just the way I am. I will elaborate on this a little later in the book, but I'm a type A personality. I'm a list guy. I'm a January baby. I'm a Capricorn. I'm a perfectionist. I easily get disappointed. But it is what drives me to be the best I can be, each day. I expect excellence in my patient outcomes, but sometimes, when bad things happen, like a wound gets infected, a joint gets stiff, or all the pain doesn't go away by my intervention, it makes me sad and makes me feel like a failure. I get very disappointed with myself and frustrated that there's nothing else I can do to make the patient better. That part of medicine stinks, but it comes with the territory, I guess.

So when things like this happen, I just say, "I'm so sorry. This is not what we were shooting for. This is not the expectation I was hoping for. I tried my best. I did my best. I don't know why you're still having some pain or why you're still a little stiff, and I'm so, so sorry I couldn't make you 100 percent better." It happens sometimes, and when it does, it's sad. I wish medicine were a perfect science. I really do. But when it's not, it's OK to say, "I'm so sorry," even when it's not our fault.

The key to being a great doctor and having a great doctor-patient relationship is owning up to problems and complications in your patients' care. You can't walk away from them. You must hold your patients' hands during these times and help them through these times. We can't just walk the mountaintops with them and desert them in the valleys. We need to be like Jesus, who said, "I will never leave you nor forsake you." We need to stand with them during the trials and tribulations of patient care and never, ever, ever neglect them. We are strongest when they are weakest. This is when they need us the most. *Never* abandon them. Help them through their complications. In the end, everyone wins. If we do not, we all lose.

CHAPTER 7

Reinvest in Your Business but Protect the Golden Goose

People who know me, and those who watched me build this business over the last twenty-five years, know that I believe, devoutly and fundamentally, in the following three principles:

1. Reinvest in your business.
2. Keep everything in-house.
3. Keep overhead down but invest in people and ancillaries that produce and generate residual income revenue sources.

Simply put, the second I recognize that I'm regularly referring patients out of Kayal Orthopaedic Center to another facility or provider because of our inability to provide that service in-house, I go on a mission to establish and build that service line center, in-house, and as soon as possible. As my practice grew over the years, I developed very strong outgoing referral patterns for all sorts of services. As an orthopaedic surgeon, we generate a lot of referrals for a lot of things. Such referrals include, but are not limited to

- bone density testing and disorders of bone metabolism referrals
- MRIs
- CT scans
- EMG/NCS
- interventional pain management referrals
- spine specialist referrals
- physical Therapy
- chiropractic
- acupuncture
- massage therapy
- podiatry consults
- custom-molded foot orthotic prescriptions
- rheumatology consults
- hand specialist referrals

And although I perform almost every type of orthopaedic surgery, I realized that I wanted to take the practice in a different direction. I wanted to develop specialty centers in the practice, dedicated to each musculoskeletal subspecialty. In doing so, I wanted to hire specialists for each center so that our patients could be seen and managed by expert master surgeons, highly trained, experienced, and sophisticated in each discipline of orthopaedic surgery.

So I did. Over the past twenty-five years, the following centers were established at Kayal Orthopaedic Center:

- Kayal Shoulder and Elbow Center
- Kayal Hand and Wrist Center

- Kayal Foot and Ankle Center
- Kayal Podiatry Center
- Kayal Hip and Knee Center
- Kayal Hip Preservation Center
- Kayal Rheumatology Center
- Kayal Osteoporosis Center
- Kayal Pain and Spine Center
- Kayal Osteoarthritis & Orthobiologics Center
- Kayal Sports Medicine
- Kayal Chiropractic
- Kayal Physical Therapy
- Kayal Robotic Joint Replacement Center
- Kayal Medical Imaging
- Kayal Laser Treatment Center
- Kayal Massage
- Kayal Acupuncture

Each had its own team of people and specialists. Each was separately developed, branded, and marketed for the unique services our highly trained and experienced specialists provide. These health care providers are the best of the best. Each was cherry-picked to further develop each individual service line at Kayal Orthopaedic Center. They were given the charge and incredible opportunity to develop a Center of Excellence and a specific niche in a booming practice. Well, needless to say, each took the ball and ran with it. And today, each of these centers within Kayal Orthopaedic Center is booming, to say the least. Almost nothing gets referred out. Remember our slogan: "Insist on excellence! Insist on Kayal Orthopaedic Center! For all of your orthopaedic needs!" We say that because everything is kept in-house, and you know what? Patients love it! They don't have to go anywhere else to see an expert. Our services are all under one roof. And because of this, all the health care providers share the same electronic health record. We have access to each other's notes, assessments, and plans, we share access to our own digital x-rays and high-resolution cross-sectional medical images (MRIs and CT scans), and we all collaborate to make our patients better and faster. If any of us needs another in-house specialist, they are available to us at our beck and call. We manage everything for our patients because it's all done in-house. We check their benefits. We get the prior authorizations. We provide the service. We see the patient back. It's a full circle of care, and it's all done in-house. There's nothing like it. That's for sure. That's what we call the Kayal Orthopaedic Center Experience.

Yes, I know all of this sounds well and good. "But how did you do it?" you ask. "All this costs lots of money, right?" Right. It does. But the money required to build this empire did not just grow on trees. It came from something that unfortunately many in recent generations don't know too much about. It's called hard work, persistence, discipline, focus, devotion, grit, dedication, commitment, and faith. All of this, thanks be to God, resulted in very good wages over the years. These good wages were then reinvested back into the practice year after year in different ways.

1. I reinvested in highly trained and experienced physicians to develop the centers described above, each with its own specialty and area of expertise.
2. I reinvested in midlevel practitioners, such as physician assistants and advanced practice nurses, both experienced ones and ones that were green and could be molded, so that they could triage patients and provide primary care orthopaedic

medicine to facilitate patient care and see patients when I was in the operating room. My philosophy has always been to let each health care provider practice to the full extent of what their licensure allows. I believe doctors should be doctors and midlevels should be midlevels. Doctors don't need to do what a midlevel can do. This allows the practice to fire on all cylinders and be the most efficient it can be. I believe so strongly in this philosophy that, as of this writing, I currently employ over twenty physician assistants and a nurse practitioner as well.

3. I continuously reinvested in ancillary sources of revenue over the years. For example, just to name a few, I purchased three MRI machines, a hospital-grade CT scanner, three bone density machines, over thirty ultrasound machines, fifteen digital x-ray machines, and built many multimillion-dollar state-of-the-art medical centers and procedure rooms clad with leaded walls for fluoroscopic-guided procedures. I also reinvested in the practice and built out gorgeous chiropractic, physical therapy, acupuncture, and therapeutic massage facilities to accommodate our patients' needs.

I guess I could have just pocketed the profits, but I chose to reinvest in myself and in my practice because I believed that I had the grit to succeed in the business of medicine and in the pursuit of the perfect doctor-patient relationship. My thought process was that for sure no one was going to guarantee a better return on investment in me than I myself would. By reinvesting my profits into my own business, I was saying to myself, "I believe in you, Rob. Yes, it's risky, but I trust and know that you can and will do this." I was not going to let myself, or my growing family at that time, down. That was for sure. And I didn't.

THE GOLDEN GOOSE

"The Golden Goose" is a classic fairy tale that has been told in various cultures. While there are different versions of the tale, the core elements typically remain the same. In one common version, there is a poor farmer who has three sons. The youngest son is often depicted as simple or foolish. One day, the youngest son is wandering in the woods when he encounters an old man who gives him a golden goose. The old man tells him that the goose will lay golden eggs. Excited by his newfound fortune, the youngest son takes the golden goose home to his family. However, when he tries to show his family the goose's ability to lay golden eggs, they are skeptical and mock him.

Despite their doubts, the golden goose indeed lays golden eggs. Word of the golden goose spreads throughout the kingdom, and soon everyone is amazed by the boy's wealth. However, the story takes a twist when people become greedy and try to steal the goose. Anyone who tries to take the goose becomes stuck to it, unable to let go.

Eventually, the youngest son sets out on a journey with the golden goose, and along the way, he encounters various characters who become stuck to the goose. These characters include a king, his daughter, and a group of musicians. Despite their initial hostility, they eventually learn to appreciate the boy's kindness and generosity. In the end, the golden goose leads the youngest son to riches, happiness, and even a royal marriage.

"The Golden Goose" teaches lessons about kindness, generosity, and the dangers of greed. It highlights the idea that true wealth comes from sharing and helping others rather than from hoarding wealth for oneself.

Well, for me, the golden goose has always been and will always be Kayal Orthopaedic Center's orthopaedic practice. It has always been what has driven this machine and has enabled it to grow and prosper. It has driven and continues to drive all sources of ancillary income for this practice and all internal referrals. No growth or expansion has ever been done or ever will be done at the expense of Kayal Orthopaedic Center's golden goose: the Department of Orthopaedic Surgery. It is protected at all costs. I challenge you to identify your golden goose, and I implore you to protect it, regardless of the cost. Without preserving its health, the growth, development, and expansion of your practice will fail. Period.

CHAPTER 8
Own and Occupy

N ow this might be a long shot, but try, if you can, to do like I have done and own the real estate that houses your medical practice(s). Why pay someone else? This follows the same principle that we previously discussed and that I feel so strongly about, which says, "Keep everything in-house." This chapter will be the shortest of them all because the concept is actually quite simple: buy your buildings personally but lease them (must be at fair market value or FMV) through your business. This way, you're owning and occupying your own property. Provided your business is not going anywhere, you maximize your write-off while enjoying a long-term lease agreement and cash flow for years to come. You're your own best tenant and landlord. I've done this repeatedly in practice, and now with so many offices in New York and New Jersey, I've built in a guaranteed long-term personal income revenue stream and real estate portfolio side business with its own business expenses. Again, why give business away to others when you can support it yourself? Given the fact that, in this day and age, you can barely even buy a single-family 4,000-square-foot home for less than $1 million (let alone a 70,000-square-foot medical center), the main problem is that most doctors frankly don't have the grit and the guts to even attempt to dabble with this. I implore you to trust yourself enough to do so. But to do so, you must follow the principles that I have tried so hard to eloquently communicate.

CHAPTER 9

Maintain a Proper Balance

I t's simple. Work hard and play hard. Be disciplined with your time. Plan. Be organized. Make things-to-do (TTD) lists. You sort of need a type A personality, like I have, to do this. Like I alluded to before, I don't know, maybe you have to be a January Capricorn baby like me. I realize for some it's not easy. However, it is if you're cut from this cloth like I am. I would argue that for people like me, it's harder to *not* be this way than it is to be this way. The problem is that people who are this way expect others to be this way, too, and we easily get disappointed when they are not like us.

This is all I know. I'm organized. I'm disciplined. I'm anal-retentive. I'm excessively orderly and fussy. I get up very early, but I go to bed by 11 p.m., too. My head usually hits the pillow at 10:30 p.m. I usually wake up at 5 or 5:30 a.m. at the latest. I can't sleep past that time. If I do, I feel like I've wasted the entire day. It kills me, and I get angry with myself. I live by my lists. I must be extremely organized. I take notes all the time. I love checking off boxes and accomplishing tasks. I follow up on everything, and I forget nothing. Please note, however, that these tasks are not all work related, although most are. Ha ha ha. Everything gets tasked. I will make boxes for everything I need to do that day, and by the end, all boxes must be checked off. They must be, or I won't go to sleep. I will make lists of things to do (TTD) each day. A typical TTD list for, say Saturday morning, includes the following:

- Read the Bible.
- Pray.
- Watch sermons.
- Do my EHR notes.
- Get caught up on emails.
- Take Luke to soccer.
- Stop at Soccer Post.
- Go through TTD lists.
- Go shopping for Christmas gifts.
- Do return at UPS.
- Work on book.
- Arrange next family vacation.
- Book flights.
- Schedule and confirm all excursions.
- Stop at Kate and Will's to see Hope.
- Dinner at Mom's with Kim and kids.
- Bible study with family at 9 p.m.

But I make those lists every day. I live by my lists. I live by my calendar. It keeps me structured and efficient. I don't like to waste any time. Not even for a minute. I must always be doing something. I must always be busy. It's just me. But I think it takes this type of personality to succeed in business and in life. At least for me it does.

For me, there is no gray area. I've always been this way. I live in the extremes. It's either black or white. I'm all in.

Just make sure you balance your personal life with your professional life. Try not to bring too much work home with you (yeah, right), although for the small business owner, that's a formidable task. Make sure that you go on vacation regularly, and while you're on vacation, make sure you're actually on vacation. That means putting away work and focusing on your family. Establish memories that will last generations. Spend the time together, and don't worry; spend the money too. The investment is priceless, and your return on this investment will be immeasurable. Try to take private excursions and trips, if possible. This will ensure that you'll spend quality one-on-one time with each other without unwanted interruptions and distractions. This will get rid of all the unwanted noise that creates great interference in relationships. Make sure that you also spend quality time, and frequently, with friends and family.

There's more to life than just work. It's important to work hard and play hard, and that is what I do. But what's more important is that you're actually a better father, mother, husband, or wife than you are a doctor or health care provider. As hard as that is for me to even think about or say, because I feel so strongly about the profession of medicine and my commitment to it, it's true. As much as I love this profession, I love God, my wife, and family much more. Always remember the following: it has to be God, then family, then work, and in that order. It must be. Any deviation from that will lead to failure, in my humble opinion. You can and should have them all, however. They are not mutually exclusive of one another. You don't need to choose one and neglect the others. You must, in fact, choose them all, but in that priority, and in that order, and you will thrive and be blessed. Trust me.

CHAPTER 10
Feeding the Sharks

O K, so here we go. We built this thing. It's jammin'. It's firing on all cylinders. Every office is bursting at the seams. Every provider's schedule is full. So things must be groovy now, right? Wrong! Everything is great, but remember what I said earlier about the dreaded increases in overhead year after year that we discussed and the payers, and their declining reimbursements, also year over year? Well, in 2021, for me, it was time to finally do something about it.

Regularly, just like most successful businesspeople, I would monitor the health of the practice. I always had my finger on the pulse with this practice. Although we were still quite profitable, like any good physician, I noticed concerning trends in the vital signs that could not be ignored. The practice was beginning to show some evidence of stress and strain. There were "early ominous EKG changes," for lack of a better analogy, and something had to be done about it. We were so busy, working so hard, but the stresses of COVID and its deleterious effects on the workforce were beginning to stress the practice a little more than I was comfortable with. After COVID, employees were asking for salaries that were previously unheard of, and the insurance companies continued to kill us with declining reimbursement rates. The "out of network" world of insurance reimbursements was finally crashing after over twenty years of threats to do so. It was finally becoming a reality and coming to fruition. I realized that the practice, in its then current form, was not sustainable. The overhead was just too much to support such a machine with evidence of a somewhat scary, downward reimbursement pattern. I needed something more sustainable. I was not willing to risk it all crashing down. I had so much invested in this practice, and I knew it was time to sell some shares and find a partner that could greatly support and strengthen the iron frame of kayalortho that was beginning to show very early signs of stress and strain. The weight and load of this large medical empire was becoming too heavy to carry alone. It was at that time that I immediately remembered the old adage used by wealth managers. "Buy low and sell high." Well, it was time.

While all of this was going on, night after night I would lie in bed before going to sleep, and I would watch *Shark Tank* with my wife. I would always tell her, "I need a shark! I should take my practice to *Shark Tank*. My practice is unique. It's unlike any other I've ever seen before. We've monopolized the area. We have every ancillary service related to musculoskeletal medicine. We occupy a humongous footprint in the New York and New Jersey Tristate area and have so many different specialists in all facets of musculoskeletal medicine. We're the best at what we do, and we offer the most cutting-edge orthopaedic technologies. And we're all under one roof! Everything is in-house. We have a one-stop shop for all of your orthopaedic needs! I want to take this model and reproduce it all over the United States of America. Doctors, in general, don't understand the business of medicine and how to be both a successful doctor and a successful businessperson at the same time. But I do!" And of course, she agreed. Ha ha ha!

So that was my next move. The rest is history. I took my practice to market. I needed a shark. I wanted an investor, but I didn't want to sell out. I wasn't looking to cash out and walk away from this monster I had built over the past twenty-five years. Rather, I was looking to keep doing what I did best and what I loved the most, and that was to continue as an orthopaedic surgeon and grow and manage the practice. But to do so, I needed a humongous partner to help provide the "strength in numbers" I so desperately desired. I needed strength and support to help me with economies of scale. I required a shark to help me negotiate the best reimbursement rates in the state through our combined size, collective numbers of lives we cared for, skill sets, excellent patient outcomes, and reputations.

So that's what I did. I went fishing and caught a shark. A great white shark. I partnered with RWJBarnabas Health, the largest health care system in New Jersey, and it has been the best move I've ever made professionally. It's been a joint-venture (JV) partnership made in heaven, which will allow us to continue to thrive in this turbulent health care milieu where so many other health care providers have been forced to throw in the towel or settle by giving up their private medical practices to hospital systems that have eaten them up like vultures. My friends and partners at RWJBarnabas Health respect the autonomy of the physicians they partner with. They became investors in our practices to help us continue to flourish by supporting us, if and when necessary. No more, no less. It's still Kayal Orthopaedic Center and I'm still the president of the organization. Now, however, I'm not alone fighting with insurance payers to allow us to care for our patients. Instead, I have the backing and support of the largest health care organization in the entire state, who has my back, advocating on behalf of our patients, and they will fight tooth and nail for them just like I would.

RWJBarnabas Health: another good and perfect gift from above. Amen, and praise the Lord.

CHAPTER 11
Faith

Well, I'm sure by now that you've appreciated some of the Christian undertones in this book. If you did, please know that they were intentional. If you didn't, I encourage you to read the Holy Bible, which is the Word of God, and get to know my awesome Triune God—God the Father, God the Son (Jesus Christ, my Lord and Savior), and God the Holy Spirit—and then you will.

Romans 1:16 says, "For I am not ashamed of the Gospel, because it is the power of God that brings salvation to everyone who believes."

The Bible tells us that God has a specific will and purpose for our lives. His Word tells us that we are also blessed with gifts from the Holy Spirit. Well, He has blessed me richly in life with so many things: a loving, faithful, supportive, devoted, and most extraordinary wife of twenty-nine years, six incredibly outstanding children, a most amazing son-in-law, our first sensational granddaughter, unbelievably marvelous parents who loved unconditionally, the most supportive, dependable, and greatest siblings anyone could ask for, the kindest and most welcoming in-laws, phenomenal friends, a

God-fearing, Bible-based Christian church, and Christian schools for our six children. And if this was not enough, He has blessed me with this outstanding practice called Kayal Orthopaedic Center and has allowed me to practice in the prestigious field of orthopaedic surgery and service thousands and thousands of patients over the past twenty-five years. Wow! He is the God of unfailing love, kindness, compassion, faithfulness, abundant grace, and mercy. His promises never fail.

God's hands are all over my life and all over this practice. This practice has been prayed for, and prayed over, for years, and without a doubt, its success and its fruits are an answer to these years of prayer to our awesome Trinity of God.

This practice is His, not mine. I work for Him. In James 1:17, the Bible says, "Every good and perfect gift is from above, coming down from the Father of heavenly lights, Who does not drift like casting shadows." This medical practice is a ministry that serves the Lord—all for His honor and glory. The Kayal Orthopaedic Center is my mission field. Through it, God has used me and our team as instruments, as vessels, to love His children, serve them, care for them, heal them, and comfort them. Over and over again, He has used us to give back to a community in need and to love our neighbors as ourselves in so many ways that are beyond the scope and purpose of the book. He has blessed this practice so that we can pay it forward and be a blessing to others.

When I go to work, I'm serving the Lord. The Bible tells us in Colossians 3:23–24, "Whatever you do, work at it with all your heart, as working for the Lord, not for human masters, since you know that you will receive an inheritance from the Lord as a reward. It is the Lord Christ you are serving."

I am so blessed to be surrounded by so many others at Kayal

Orthopaedic Center who have the same love for others and the same hearts for people.

Yes, He has blessed me. But He has blessed me because He knows that I know from whom all these blessings flow. He knows that He can trust me to be a good steward of His provisions. Remember the Bible tells us in Luke 16:10, "Whoever can be trusted with very little can also be trusted with much, and whoever is dishonest with very little will also be dishonest with much." Furthermore, He also tells us in Matthew 25:29, "For whoever has will be given more, and they will have an abundance. Whoever does not have, even what they have will be taken from them."

Well, as far as I'm concerned, "as for me and this house, we will serve the Lord" (Joshua 24:15).

CONCLUSION

Well, at this point, I don't know what else to say. I think I've said everything that I've wanted to say. I have wanted to write this book for a few years now. It's actually been on my TTD list for at least five years. I'm so glad that I can now finally strike a line across this one. You have no idea how good that makes me feel.

Anyway, I really hope that this book will help you fulfill all your professional goals in this spectacular field of medicine that we both get to call our own. Look. You've worked so hard to get where you are. I'm so glad you took the time to read this book. Personally, I think every medical school student and every resident, physician assistant, nurse practitioner, chiropractor, physical therapist, acupuncturist, massage therapist, and every other health care provider in every field of medicine should read this book before they go out into the real world, treat patients, and attempt to build a successful medical practice. In fact, I firmly believe it should be a mandatory read in every single training program, not only across the United States of America but across the world. And frankly, the fact of the matter is they just don't teach us any of this stuff during our ten years of training after we graduate from college. We're just expected to learn it and master it on our own. And most, by far, never do. They never even come close. And for those who do, by the time they finally get it or learn it, it's time for them to retire.

This formula works. I've perfected it and figured it all out already. I've reproduced this repeatedly in my career, and each and every time, praise be to God, everything I have touched has turned to gold. It's because I know how to do it. And even I, as an orthopaedic surgeon who fixes things for a living, don't need to fix something if it's not broken. So, I don't. I just reproduce it, scale it, and grow it, and God-willing, I'll continue to do this for many more years. I have mastered the business of medicine and the doctor-patient relationship. Just as the recipe for Coca-Cola remains a closely guarded trade secret, I own the recipe for success in medicine and I'm not going to mess with it. I only wish to use it to help you achieve all the goals you desired when you embarked out on your professional career in medicine. As I have said, this formula works. It works for me, and it should work for you. But if it doesn't, let me know. Perhaps I can help you. And certainly, if you run a complementary practice in the New York and New Jersey Tristate area and you are looking for your shark, perhaps you can become a bolt on to our train. Just reach out. I would be happy to talk to you.

I put my heart and soul into writing this book. Thoughts and words just flowed and spewed from my brain to my fingers and then to the computer's Microsoft Word document without ceasing. I couldn't type fast enough. In fact, I wrote this nearly 26,000-word book in just a couple of days.

I didn't have to research any of this except for the few statistics I've mentioned, because it's all in my brain, and on my heart. I speak from my heart. I hope you listen to me and meditate on the thoughts and principles I've outlined. They're *all* important and *all* critical to your success.

Always remember what I said. It's first and foremost God, then family, and then work—in that order.

Don't ever compromise that.

Now crush it.

Peace.

Robert A. Kayal, MD, FAAOS, FAAHKS
Kayal Orthopaedic Center
Founder, president, and CEO
rkayalmd@kayalortho.com

ABOUT THE AUTHOR

Robert A. Kayal, MD, FAAOS, FAAHKS, is the founder, president, and CEO of Kayal Orthopaedic Center located in northern New Jersey and New York. Dr. Kayal is the husband of Kim S. Kayal, RN, and father of their six children: Katlyn Madeline, Michaela Noel, Robert Joseph, Shannon Isabella, Mia Grace, and Luke Christopher. Dr. Kayal is the proud grandfather (Gido) of their newest family addition, Hope Madeline.

During the last twenty-five years, Dr. Kayal built one of the most successful multispecialty orthopaedic medical practices in the United States, and in 2021, in one of the most substantial health care transactions ever to close, he partnered with RWJBarnabas Health, the largest and most comprehensive health care system in New Jersey.

Dr. Kayal considers it an honor, pleasure, blessing, and privilege to help restore an active lifestyle and joyful life to each of his patients. He gives all his thanks to God for his talents and skills and prays his practice will always be used to honor, glorify, and exalt his awesome Triune God: God the Father, God the Son, and God the Holy Spirit.

Printed in the USA
CPSIA information can be obtained
at www.ICGtesting.com
LVHW050823300524
781584LV00005B/75/J

9 798385 023905